Parenting You. ....

The Essential and Practical Guide to Raising Children to Become Their Best

By John Adjei

CONTENTS

Introduction

Foreword

This special and wonderful book on effective and successful parenting, which is raising and nurturing your children to become their best, is indeed, a well-researched practical guide that must be a much coveted manual in the library of every family.

As a parent of three children himself – aged 7, 10, and 12 years – John knows only too well the frustrations and challenges that every parent faces. It was in fact his worst experience as a parent that led him to research and write this book. In these pages you will find an overview of the existing expert research on parenting and child psychology, illustrated by examples from his own life.

Throughout this book with its attractive and well layout format, John shows how to be both strong and loving when children need it most – that is, at the very times when they have worn your patience thin. He has included his own experiences of the common challenges, pitfalls, and misunderstandings that most parents will face at some point. These are accompanied by clearly-marked tips and insights to help you identify the root of the problem, and to guide you through an appropriate response.

You will also find brief summaries, worksheets, and goal-setting templates, informed by his years as an educator, and a great deal of practical, heartfelt advice. The core of this book is a set of very simple but a comprehensive guide and very effective steps that you can begin taking today.

I can confidently predict the effect on the children of everyone who studies and applies the great principles outlined in this book. They and society will indeed be blessed.'

Rev Edwin Donkor
(ICGC Regional Overseer, Europe and North America)

What others are saying about the book

'Just wow!!! It is very, very practical, which is what everyone needs. [...] a must-have for every parent and every educational institution to learn how to raise up children to become their best.'
Nkiru Ojimadu (Author, speaker and coach)

'Your story made me cry [...] I think you are right in pointing out that because of the Act, parenting is different for the current generation of parents. We are the generation caught in between, as we were brought up being caned, but now we have to bring up our children without the cane [...] thought-provoking and has made me reflect more on what parenting means.'
P. Wendelkin (Educator and parent)

'It's not just a book only for raising children but for raising parents up to the task of parenting.'
Anita Addae (Nurse and parent)

'This book needs to be every parent and carer's holy book. Thank you for being selfless and empowering us with your personal experience [...] I believe this world will have a much better future generation because of this book.'
Afua Boateng-Addo (Accountant and parent)

'This book contains lots of treasures for parents and guardians'
Ernest Moses (Youth coach and parent)

'The ideas espoused in this book about parenting are epic and sensational! These well-researched, informative, and brilliant materials provide such practical guidance on parenting from a real-life situation, the like of which has never been seen before. As a parent, there was that real resonance when I read the book and I can say without equivocation that, my approach to parenting will never be the same. The way this book is written is indeed, a novelty and can only come from an author with great deal of ingenuity. Great work from a great Author!'
Peter Frimpong Manso (Writer and Parent).

Also, there are many 5-star reviews about this book on Amazon.co.uk and Amazon.com that can be checked by the following link: https://getBook.at/AmazonJA

Why I wrote this book

I wrote this book out of desperation, when I was looking for answers to many questions I had as a parent of three children. These problems were compounded by an extremely difficult situation in my family. My desperation sent me on a voyage to discover the essential keys for successful parenting.

The story of that bumpy journey, the discoveries I made through trial and error, and how I learned to apply those lessons without giving up is what you are holding in your hands.

Parenting is the most difficult job I have ever had. I have been through the school of hard knocks, and in the absence of other choices, I learnt some things the hard way. Going through what I did was not easy, and it was not easy to write about. It has taken me a lot of courage to grant you access to the most difficult and vulnerable moments in my parenting life.

But I want to share my experiences with other families all over the world, so that it may offer them hope and help strengthen the loving relationships in their homes. When I was struggling, I would have liked to find a book based on a true story of parenting. There seem to be so few parenting manuals out there inspired by actual personal and practical experiences. By sharing my story with you, I hope to pass on these valuable lessons for raising happy, confident, resilient, and responsible children within a supportive family environment.

I also realised that there was a gap in the market for parenting books. It was hard to find in one place a book that addresses all aspects of a child's growth: their physical, psychological, and spiritual dimensions or needs. Most of the experts in this field are psychologists and approach parenting from psychological perspectives, with no attention paid to the spiritual side of the child. This book acknowledges both the human and divine aspects of children and makes suggestions on how to address those needs to raise a balanced and holistic child, who has both emotional and spiritual intelligence in addition to their IQ. This book is still relevant to parents who don't believe in the Divine.

By sharing my message, I hope it may resonate with other parents. I hope they find inspiration in the thoughts expressed here, and that this book helps them avoid my own mistakes and become better parents. I hope that my story, my practical experiences, and my lessons will encourage other parents to have the courage to try, try, and try again, and see the potential transformation that can happen when we choose our responses carefully.

Some of the themes I will address here – corporal punishment, how to deal with your own failure – are difficult to discuss. But if I have learned one thing from my own journey as a parent, it is that painful experiences are not necessarily destructive. They can be extremely useful, as long as we approach them in the right way – with humility, and a willingness to learn from them.

Why am I so passionate about this? Personally, I cannot put a price on helping parents make a more positive impact in the lives of their children. This not only helps create peace and harmony in the home, but it ripples outwards to touch our communities, our cities, and our country, eventually making this world a better place for all. It is simply invaluable work to be doing, and I feel privileged to be a part of doing it.

Why should you read this book?

This book is for anyone looking for a calmer, easier and happier relationship with people, particularly children. It is for any parent who has ever struggled – which is all of us, at one time or another. Perhaps you may be doing reasonably fine but just want to be better and raise your children or any child under your influence to be their best.

Do you want to raise your children to be their most extraordinary selves?

Do you struggle to get your children to cooperate with you?

Do you want to help your children grow and discover themselves, but you're not sure how to go about it?

This book holds the answers to all these questions and more. For parents with children aged 0-18 years, it's designed to offer practical step-by-step guidance, along with a range of techniques, tools and activities to help your children become their very best selves. This book is also intended to equip you to be your best, too – to raise yourself up, in the selfless pursuit to raise your children.

As a parent, you don't have to be the very best, but you can try to be better. Everyone can try.

Every child is special. Often, they just need a little guidance to help them reach their full potential.

This book will inspire you to make some simple but profound changes in how you approach parenting. And if you do, you can expect both better outcomes and a better relationship with your children, one that you can be proud of.

How to get the most from this book

This book is intended to be treated as a reference manual. It contains 7 Chapters and 7 Strategies, along with activities for parents to try. You are encouraged to revisit it regularly, particularly those sections you find most relevant to your own circumstances.

As a parent, you have a greater chance of getting the most from this book by making notes as you go along, and then applying the ideas contained here to your own life. The recommended activities and exercises at the end of each chapter will help you to truly understand the strategies and principles for helping your children, right from birth through their toddler and discovery years, until they are safely past their teens. A helpful goal-setting template is also included for each learnable technique or tool.

You are strongly encouraged to attempt these exercises and templates yourself, in order to take the ideas from this book and transform it into powerful experiential knowledge. If you do, I promise that you will see a change in your parenting skills, and in how you approach your relationship with your children.

Are you ready to lead, and become a better role model for your child? If so, then I invite you to read on.

Chapter 1: My Story, and the Lessons I Learned

In this chapter, you will be introduced to:

- My story

- The lessons

- Activities for parents

- Goal-setting template

- My story and its lessons in a nutshell

My story

Prior to experiencing one of our most difficult moments as parents, my wife Linda and I had thought we were excellent parents.

We had three beautiful, exuberant, and delightful children. Each morning after waking up, they would come into our room to say, 'Hello Dad! Hello Mum!' We would embrace them warmly, starting the day on a high note. I would get up and help them brush their teeth. Their mother would help them get dressed for school, or whatever else the day held, while I would make their breakfast. Then they would go off to school and Linda and I to work.

Later, Linda would be there to pick them up from school and keep them safe and happy until my return. I would arrive home to an exciting welcome and lots of hugs: 'Hello Daddy!' Then I would help them with their homework and keep them entertained with stories until it was bedtime.

In short, we thought we were on top of our game and doing exceptionally well as parents. Our children were generally happy and we had no cause to worry. Looking after them could be challenging and sometimes stressful, but the experience was mostly wonderful. We were admired and treated with a great deal of respect by other parents of young children.

This continued until our three children were 4, 7 and 9 years old. Until then, we had relied on the knowledge and skills handed down to us by our parents, embedded in their own culture and history, along with some Christian values and principles.

This skill-set was put to the test enormously when our children began to behave like 'typical' children – asking questions, displaying challenging behaviour, copying their friends, and essentially acting exactly like any normal, average child in the UK.

A 'reasonable punishment' by smacking was our main disciplinary tool. We didn't know any better than that. This is what our parents had done when we were children, and since we had turned out fine, we thought we had discovered the key to discipline and successful parenting. Smacking our own children on the back of the hand was an automatic and immediate punishment for bad behaviour. It never even occurred to us something was not right with this.

As time went on, smacking as a form of punishment gradually became ineffective. The children would only laugh at us, knowing that we did it in love and care. *What can I do next?* I asked myself. I remembered how my parents had used the cane, as generations before them had done. In fact, the use of the cane as a means of discipline has eaten into the fabric of society in most countries in the developing world, including Ghana. It is used in schools even today, and is still very common in remoter parts of the country. I was brought up in Ghana, and lived there until after completing my bachelor's degree. And so, in my mind, the use of the cane was utterly normal.

The moment of regret

I soon found myself warning and threatening my children with the belt. I told them that it would be used to strike their hand if any bad behaviour was demonstrated, or if I wanted to stop any unacceptable behaviour. This threat – though with no intention to carry it through – was my last resort when all that I knew about parenting proved woefully ineffective in getting my children to do what we wanted them to do.

At first, the threat appeared to work as a deterrent. This went on for more than a year without my ever using the belt. But as the children gradually understood that Dad would never follow through on his threat, this also lost its effectiveness as a deterrent over time.

One day, when my wife was away, the children managed to push virtually all of my buttons. I became so angry that I ended up striking one of them (the main 'culprit') with the belt, telling her, 'I will beat the devil out of you today.' I gave her one measured stroke on her palm, making sure it did not leave any mark or bruise on her.

My goodness! I thought afterwards. *What have I done? Is this discipline or the misapplication of it?* I began to question myself: *is it because you are bigger than them and they cannot strike back? Are you taking advantage of their weakness and vulnerability? Where is the love? Where is the care? Where is the compassion?*

These thoughts and others began to flood my mind. I felt awful. And so I mustered the courage to apologise to them and promised never to use the belt again.

However, that incident appeared to leave indelible emotional wounds on my children. Acts that inflict physical or emotional pain in the name of discipline or punishment prove to be counterproductive. They actually erode the love, connection and bond between us as parents and our children.

Our children began to become more angry towards us. My relationship with them was never the same again. They became suspicious, fearful, and intimidated. These were the last things I wanted as an outcome of my parenting.

One morning, over a month after this belt incident, my daughter was irritable and unhappy at school, complaining that her parents were always shouting at her. Her teachers spotted this as unusual behaviour in a child who had previously been so happy. They called her to one side and assured her that that she should feel comfortable telling them anything. They promised to provide a safe and protective environment if she was honest with them and explained what was going on.

According to my daughter, she then told them about the belt incident – though with some exaggerations and embellishments, making it appear as if the use of the belt was a daily occurrence in our house. My daughter felt that she had to fabricate things as a way to exorcise her anger towards us.

She had no idea the consequences her actions would have. Social Services were quickly called in, as the teachers quite rightly have a duty of care to refer a case like this for intervention, in order to safeguard and protect the child.

The moment of consequence

At this point, I genuinely didn't know the severity and seriousness of that one action of mine. I sincerely did not know that using a belt to strike a child was a criminal offence. My understanding was that so long as the intention was not to harm and the disciplinary action was reasonable, proportionate, and did not cause a bruise or mark on the body of the child, it was fine.

I had no idea that using any object including a belt was against the law, according to the UK's Children Act of 1989. So when I received a call from my wife on my way home from work, telling me that someone from Social Services was waiting for me, I had nothing to worry about. I arrived home and warmly greeted the young lady. What followed was this conversation:

Social worker: 'Hi, my name is _____ and I'm a social worker. We had a report from your child's school and I am here to find out more information.'

Me: 'Oh, thank you for coming.'

Social worker: 'Did you use the belt on your daughter, _____ ?'

Me: 'Yes...'

Social worker: 'Why is that?'

Me: '… I did and wanted to teach her a lesson about not lying.'

Social worker: 'Did you tell your wife?'

Me: 'No.'

Social worker: 'Why not?'

Me: 'I did not tell my wife because I did not consider this a big deal. It was a once off and I promised them it would never happen again, and it has not happened again.'

Social worker: 'Your daughter says it is not once-off thing.'

Me: 'Can I ask my daughter to confirm this?'

The social worker appeared to ignore this question. Instead, she called her boss for advice, and then began to threaten me.

Social worker: 'I was going to take these three children away, but it is too late to arrange for school tomorrow morning for them. But you have to leave the house, get somewhere to spend the night to enable us to investigate before you can come back.'

Of course, my answers to all her questions were without any awareness of the law. I was not aware of the gravity of my actions. This, combined with the social worker's attitude – she did not appear to be sure of what she was doing, as she had to call her supervisor approximately three times for guidance during our conversation – made me conclude that she was either an impostor or that she was very inexperienced.

My understanding, even now, is that a professional social worker should first seek to serve the holistic interests of the family. Nothing in our interaction that day suggested that she was offering us support. From my perspective, she seemed only to want to destroy our family.

So there was a fundamental misunderstanding between us. I was left wondering what I had done that could be so serious as to stop me from sleeping in my own house or to have my children taken away from me.

In this moment of uncertainty, not knowing whether or not she was genuinely a social worker putting me in the position of a serious offender, I ended up calling the police myself.

Me: 'Hello, my name is John. I have got a social worker here threatening me with having to leave my house.'
Once the police heard that social services were in my house, they did not want to even listen to why I was calling.

Police: 'Can I take a few details from you?'

Me: 'Sure.'

Once he had taken all my details – my full name, date of birth, address, and so on – I thought he was ready to listen to me.

Police: 'Can you pass me on to the social worker?'

Me: 'Won't you hear why I called you?'

The Police: 'Pass me over to the social worker.'

This is not fair, I thought to myself. I was shocked and confused. It took a lot of my strength not to hang up the phone. I put the phone on speaker mode and handed it over, as asked. I was even more shocked to hear what the social worker then told the police.

> **Social worker**: '… John doesn't realise he has broken the law [here she quoted the exact section of The Children Act 1989 that prohibits the use of any object to strike a child]. I have asked him to leave the house and he has refused.'

> **Me**: [interrupting] 'This is not true!'

> **Police**: 'Do you want me to record this as a criminal case?'

> **Social worker**: 'Yes.'

> **Police**: 'Do you want me to send officers to get him out?'

> **Social worker**: 'Sure!'

She then was given the reference number for the criminal case, and requested police personnel to be dispatched to kick me out of my house.

I was dumbfounded by her sheer misrepresentation of my statements, and how the police seemed unwilling to even listen to what I had to say. It also began to dawn on me in that moment the seriousness of what I had done.

The moment of despair

After hearing what the social worker had told the police, my children burst into tears and began screaming. Mum was also crying, the children were confused and frightened, Mum was perplexed, Dad was bewildered and anxious – the family was in utter chaos and facing huge uncertainty.

Several questions were running through my mind: *What will happen? Will I be handcuffed? Will I go to jail? Who will help*

Linda look after the children? What happens to our children? Who will pay the mortgage? Does this offence mean I cannot work with anyone below the age of 18 in the UK? If so, I would not even be able carry out my profession, as I sometimes teach a university preparation course and some of my students are minors (under 18 years of age).

The chaos made the social worker leave the house, leaving us in limbo while she called her boss about what had transpired.

While waiting, I called my pastor in desperation. He gave me the contact of an experienced social worker. This social worker explained to me that it was okay to smack a child, but unlawful to use any object to do so. I am not sure why the thought of calling these people first for help did not occur to me earlier. Perhaps, if the young (apparently trainee) social worker had clearly explained the situation and approached it in a reasonable tone, things may have not ended up the way they did.

I also went to our next-door neighbour and confided in her about what had happened. She called her husband for advice. She also promised to let me sleep in her house for the night. Thankfully, the manager from social services arrived first. She had a long chat with her young colleague in their car, just outside our house.

Then she came inside, quickly registered the atmosphere, and asked a few questions. All this time our last child, who was only 4 at the time, had jumped on to my lap and was holding me tightly, not wanting to let me go anywhere.

Social Services Manager: 'Who called the police?'

Me: 'I did.'

Social Services Manager: 'Call them again for me, I need to talk to them.'

Not again, I thought. But I did as she asked.

Social Services Manager: 'Hello, I am _____ , calling regarding case with reference number _____ .'

Police: 'How can I help you?'

Social Services Manager: 'I am calling to cancel this case.'

Police: 'Why?'

Social Services Manager: 'I have a strategy to solve the issue.'

At that, I breathed a huge sigh of relief.

Then the neighbours told the manager that they were willing to vouch for me, because they had known me to be a good person and a good parent and we often babysat for each other. I was pleasantly surprised by their willingness and their desire to help me. What a show of love in a difficult situation!

The social services manager took her time to calmly and reasonably explain things to me. She advised me to leave the house until the evening of the next day, and told me that I could not stay within a certain distance of the house, so unfortunately my neighbours offer could not be taken up.

I ended up in a bed and breakfast, and left from there to go to work the next morning. After work, I returned to stand outside in the cold waiting for social services to arrive first. I waited for two hours. Later, we discovered that the social worker's car had broken down and a new person had to be called in to cover them. The wait was an extremely anxious one. I was freezing and deeply upset, and I did not know what was going to happen next.

Eventually, two people arrived to speak to my wife and I.

They introduced us to acceptable ways to discipline our children: reasonable smacking with the hand (not above the neck, and not with an object), timeout, and other methods. They told us that the case would be investigated further and could take up to six months to do so. In the meantime, while the investigations were underway, they told us that we should agree on and sign that we would adhere to the following stipulations:

- Not to use physical chastisement towards any of the children in the future, but explore different discipline methods to use on them

- To allow checks to be completed with relevant professionals such as the family doctor (GP), and teachers from the children's school

- To work in partnership with the allocated Social Worker from Children's Services and other professionals involved in the protection of the children

- To make ourselves available for visits with Children's Services

- Not to punish the children because of the disclosures that had been made in relation to physical chastisement, otherwise the Local Authority may wish to seek legal advice to secure the immediate safety of the children.

When the two people from Social Services left, I hugged my daughter and assured her of my love. 'I still love you,' I told her. 'You did not do anything wrong. You did not know what would happen.' Even I, in spite of my education and training in safeguarding children and young people, had not known.

The moment of hope

About four months later, when picking up the children from school, my wife Linda met with the first social worker who had arrived to intervene at our house.

Social worker: 'Hi, Linda, how are you?'

Linda: 'I am fine, thank you.'

Social worker: [*gently*] 'I called you on your mobile phone, and I knocked at your door this morning, but there was no answer.'

Linda: 'Oh, no! Let me check my phone call logs. I don't seem to have received any missed call today, though. What number did you call?

Social worker: 'Don't worry, I must have called a different number.'

Linda: 'We have been waiting to hear from you.'

Social worker: 'Can we have a brief chat in my car?'

Linda: 'Yes, provided there is enough room for the children as well.'

Social worker: 'I came to this school to speak to the children and their teachers for more information. The teachers have not raised any concerns about the progress and welfare of the children. Similarly, the GP has not raised any health concern regarding any of the children.'

Linda: 'Oh, that is what I would expect, thank you.'

Social worker: 'Do you have any questions you may want to ask me?'

Linda: 'No!'

Social worker: 'You will hear from us in writing in a few weeks. If you happen to have any queries, please do get in touch with me'

Linda: 'Thank you.'

A couple of months later, the long-awaited letter arrived through the post with the following outcome and notes:

A – No Further Action. The parents have signed a working agreement stating that they will refrain from using any objects to hit the children. The parents have engaged with the Children's Social Care. The Parents appeared to be remorseful for their actions. Since the referral, the school has not raised any further concerns.

Three years after this incident, however, I was still grappling with the indelible rift it had left my relationship with my daughter. Imagine how you would feel if some years after such an episode your child tells you, 'Dad, when you say you love me, I don't think that I deserve it.'

It came as a shock to me, as I had always reassured her that she did the right thing, and I had continued to show my unconditional love towards her.

Things are far better now between us. In hindsight, I am immensely heartened by the courage and strength we demonstrated in sticking together as a family, and the brave way that we weathered this storm. The wonderful achievements of our children at school continue to surprise me. For example, in their academic studies, each one is performing above expectations. They are also very active in extra-curricular activities. One of them is a captain of their school's netball team. Two of them have even won the X-Factor singing competition in their primary school! They are happy, confident, independent, and purposeful.

Today, I can look back and smile. But it was a defining moment in our lives, and it forever changed how I look at parenting.

The lessons

The painful experience my family and I went through has taught me a number of key lessons and principles about parenting. This is what inspired me to write this book to help other parents – I want parents to know that regardless of the difficulties they might encounter, there is hope. We all have different parenting challenges, but irrespective of your unique circumstances, you will find at least some of the lessons and the ideas in this book useful in dealing with them. I feel passionately about this topic. I want to do whatever it takes to ensure that other parents can avoid the problems I had to go through, an experience which had the potential to destroy the relationship I had with my children and family.

The **three most crucial lessons** I learned were:

- Ignorance is the root cause of almost all parenting problems.

- Every cloud has a silver lining.

- Nothing changes until we take full responsibility for what has happened.

There is a lot of wisdom contained in each of these lessons. Each one could have a whole book dedicated to it, in fact. But for the purposes of brevity, I will explore each of them in the section below.

Lesson 1: Ignorance is the root cause of almost all parenting problems

Ignorance is basically a lack of information or lack of knowledge in any given area. Ignorance equates to simply this:

'I don't know'.

We are all ignorant to varying degrees about different areas of life. No one knows everything. It is this lack of awareness, information or knowledge that makes us do damaging things that are not in the best interest of our children, usually with good and sincere intentions.

Ignorance is not bliss. Rather, ignorance has the potential to destroy us and our relationships with those we love most. So when it comes to parenting, ignorance should be seen as the number one enemy. It needs to be defeated at all costs. I had to admit the painful truth that I did not know it all, and that the level of knowledge I was operating from was woefully inadequate and not fit for purpose. I needed to be more knowledgeable about more things concerning parenting, and to make a decision and a commitment to do whatever it took to put my new knowledge into action.

There are many areas in which parents can be better informed. These include:

a) The purpose of parenting

I am reminded of the famous quote by Dr Myles Munroe: 'When purpose is not known, abuse is inevitable'.[1]

This statement can be applied to so many aspects of life, including parenting. Many parents may be ill-informed about what exactly parenting is and their reason for doing it. Some parents may think of their role as just being about providing food, clothes, shelter, and sending the child to school and paying for their expenses. Many children are born because

---

[1] From Myles Munroe (2001), *Understanding the Purpose and Power of Woman*, New Kensington, Whitaker House.

parents want to show off, make their lives complete, have a family, or for other selfish motives. In this case, a child is used as an accessory or as a tool to satisfy the desires of the parents without any attention being paid to the purpose from the child's perspective. When this happens, abuse is almost unavoidable.

In my case and in my obliviousness, I realised my actions were in line with the parenting style I had inherited from my own upbringing and how I myself was 'parented'. It appeared as if I was abusing my power and authority, in an attempt to provide a loving, caring, respectful and a happy family atmosphere. I will speak more about this in Chapter 2, under '**Understanding the child's heart cry and mindset**'.

b) The civil laws

When it comes to the laws governing a country or society, ignorance of the law is no excuse. In my case, I was ignorant of the interpretation of some sections of the UK's Act of Parliament regarding children, **the Children Act 1989**, which has subsequently been partly amended in **the Children Act 2004**.

I was shocked to realise that one can hear about the law and still be ignorant about its contents. Parents need to be aware of the essential regulations and laws establishing the boundaries of parenting, or what parents can do and cannot do in their country of residence. For more information, please refer to Chapter 4 under the subheading, '**What is wrong with punishment as a method of discipline?**'

c) The emotional needs of the child

Besides their basic physical needs, such as food, clothes, warmth, shelter, and so on, children also have emotional needs that drive most of their behaviour. They need love, affection, to be heard, to be respected, and for their feelings to be acknowledged. These needs are essential requirements for children. They are needed in varying degrees for different age groups. There are more details on this in Chapters 4 and 5, and in the '**Age-specific parenting tips**' in Chapter 7.

Lesson 2: Every cloud has a silver lining

Another positive lesson that emerged from my story was the realisation that painful experiences are not necessarily destructive. The pain from my moment of distress, when I was removed from my family, gave me the opportunity to reflect on my actions and what I could do differently in future.

In this fast-paced world, most people are living their lives in a way that does not allow them time to pause, stop, and listen to themselves. This, coupled with the challenges of parenting, leads to exhaustion. It leaves us completely drained, stressed beyond our endurance with no inner strength left to enable us to handle the problems our children throw at us.

Sometimes, it takes a painful experience to force us to slow down, reflect and to restart with fresh energy and perspective. Our desperation in moments of pain compels us to sit down, be still, ask questions, and seek answers from within.

It would not have even occurred to me that I needed more knowledge if I had not gone through this painful, unforgettable experience. We all have painful times and the key is to heed the lesson to be learned. A painful experience, coupled with a reflection, backed by a positive action leads to progress in any endeavour. This can actually be mathematically expressed as:

$$P * R * A = P$$
Pain x Reflection x Action = Progress

This algebraic expression has enormous interpretation and implications. It implies that progress is the product or the interplay of pain (1st P), reflection (R) and a corresponding action (A) stemming from the reflection. If one of these components is not present (expressed as zero), the result of the equation is nil (also zero). That is, no progress (2nd P) in life can be expected, and we become stuck.

This profound, yet simple, model has a general application across our lives: in parenting, marriage, business, politics, and every other sphere of life. Do you have moments when you feel like nothing is working? We all feel stuck at some stage. When this happens, it is time to critically evaluate, think, ponder, reflect and then take action. In our pondering and reflection, great lessons emerge and ideas are formed, which lead to action to propel us forward in the right direction.

Does this mean that we *need* a painful experience in order to make progress? No. Although most people are not motivated to make any positive changes without some discomfort or pain, this pain doesn't necessarily have to be your own personal pain. The painful experiences of others that we pick up through observation can also help us, if we look at them with the right attitude and are willing to learn the key lessons.

This model also helps us to generally see problems and hardships in parenting or in life in the right perspective. Difficulties are necessary for progress. There is no invention or innovation that did not come out of an attempt to solve a problem or alleviate some pain or to make life a little better for people. There are many examples of this, from social media to medicine, and from education to entertainment.

If I had been given the benefit of the doubt by the professionals who intervened in our situation, it would not have prompted me to write this book you are reading. That is a positive that came out of a negative. I urge you to see the silver lining in all the apparent disappointments you experience in your parenting endeavours.

With this model in mind, we are able to turn our pain into a treasure to benefit all of humanity – or, at the very least, those people who are experiencing similar problems and challenges. This book is a testament to this idea that any painful experience is not necessarily destructive. It only remains painful when we do not reflect and take the necessary action.

Lesson 3: Nothing changes until I take full responsibility for what has happened

As no parent is 100% perfect, we are bound to make a number of mistakes on our parenting journey.

However, every parent must be wise enough to admit their own imperfections and missteps, to learn and profit from their mistakes, and be strong enough to confront and correct them. Success in parenting requires parents to take 100% responsibility for their actions and inactions.

In my own case, I could have blamed the police. I could have put all the blame on the 'inexperienced' social worker, or even on the teachers who raised the alarm and triggered the intervention process. I could also have blamed my innocent child.

But these are all excuses or attempts to avoid taking full responsibility to confront the problem. We are not willing to either improve or change what we are not willing to confront by taking responsibility. In his book, *The Success Principles*, Jack Canfield[2] illustrates the power of being responsible (or response-able) for determining the results we have in our lives and relationships. He uses a profoundly simple model to illustrate this:

E + R = O
Events + Response = Outcome

---

[2] From Jack Canfield (2005), *The Success Principles*, New York, HarperCollins: p 6.

This equation or formula simply shows that any result or outcome we have in our lives is determined by two forces: the events (what happens to us), and the actions (what we do in response to these events).

In my story, the actions taken by the professionals – such as the social workers, the school teachers, the police – along with the behaviour of my child, the laws, and other factors, were the events (E). These we usually have little or no control over.

But these are not the only factors in the equation to determine the final outcome or result. The most significant and influential element in the formula for success in any endeavour is our response (R) to what happens to us. The good news is that we have absolute control over our response. We can choose to respond to our children's most difficult and challenging behaviour in a way that influences that most important outcome: our relationship with them, and who they ultimately become. In my case, I chose the path of humility, love, compassion, empathy, sacrifice, and diligence, as the motivation for my response to these events.

Have you had events happen to you which seem difficult to bear or let go of, or which appear grossly unfair? If we do not choose the right response, these events can leave us drained, bitter, and exhausted. The truth is that those events don't determine the final outcome of our relationship with our children. They will do so only if we do not respond at all, or respond with no proven practical parenting skills, tools or strategies, such as those shared in this book. In parenting, we all have those moments that make us think, 'There is nothing I can do.' However, the power to turn things around is always, and will always be, in our response to those events. The power to do it is inside of us. The questions to ask are:

- Are we or are you willing to learn the skills?

- Are you willing to pay the price to put those skills into action?

If your answer to both questions is yes, better results can be assured, success can be expected, and your parenting outcomes can be predictable with a high degree of certainty.

Activities for parents

Below are some activities you can try, to internalise this idea that while you do not have control over the events that occur in your life, you can control your responses.

Some of the behaviours by or events with my child that make me upset are:

- ....
....

- ....
....

- ....
....

My usual response/reaction to these events has been:

- ....
....

- ....
....

- ....
....

The new responses/reactions I am going to try are:

- ....
....

- ....
....

John Adjei

- ....
  ....

Review after one week, and after one month. How did my child's behaviour change?

- ....
  ....

- ....
  ....

- ....
  ....

This principle may take a while to work for your child, so be patient. Keep on trying new ways of responding, until you find what works for you. Alternatively, you may find the goal-setting template below useful:

Goal-setting template

What do I want? (State the goal clearly, making it specific)	Why do I want this?	What can I do every day to move a step towards achieving the goal?	How and by when do I want to achieve this goal?

My story and its lessons in a nutshell

My experience, and the lessons I learned from it, have made me more aware that parenting is a journey, one that most of us embark on without much preparation. As no parent is perfect, we will all make mistakes and errors of judgement along the way.

One of the wonderful things about children is that they almost always give you a second chance. As long as you are willing to acknowledge and learn from these (usually unintended) mistakes, there is hope for your relationship with your child, and a better outcome can be expected.

As parents, we need to be informed: about parenting, the law, and our children. We also need to accept that painful experiences can actually help us to ask questions, and seek answers from within. And we need to take responsibility for our actions, or we will never improve or change.

It is only when parents are not willing to pay the price of learning and applying their new knowledge that the situation can turn into despair. The fact that you are reading this book is a clear sign that you are willing to do this, and are in fact already taking the first step. Congratulations! You are in the top tier of all parents in the world.

This chapter also highlighted the importance of our responses and reactions to what our children do or what happens to us on our journey. The truth is that parents have the power to choose their response to any given situation, and can in this way influence the outcome. Your response, positive or negative, can either make matters better or worse. It is all in your hands. Positive reactions to unpleasant parenting events can help turn the situation around for all concerned.

Notes

Chapter 2: The Fundamentals of Parenting

In this chapter, you will be introduced to:

- Understanding the child's 'heart cry' and mindset

    - What is the purpose of parenting?

    - How can we raise a child whose future is predictable?

    - What do the parenting experts say?

- The essential need for love (dignity, respect and honour)

    - Why is demonstrating love so important to your child?

    - A note on parenting styles

- Activities for parents

- Goal-setting template

- The fundamentals of parenting in a nutshell

Understanding the child's 'heart cry' and mindset

It was a Sunday morning when my wife, Linda, began to feel very different. She had successfully carried our baby for the last nine months, and now her 'water' had broken. Mum to be had to be taken to the hospital!

There the anxious wait began – at least on my part, as I sat by my wife's bedside. We waited throughout the night, but the baby seemed not to be coming. The pain on Linda's face, having laboured for almost 24 hours, was becoming increasingly unbearable. Then, out of the blue, the midwife shouted, 'Good news! The baby's head is out.' By then, Linda appeared to have expended all her energy and to have no strength left to push further. But somehow, she miraculously managed through excruciating pain to try again. Suddenly, there was our baby, crying loudly: *'Nehhhhhh! Nehhhhhh!'*

Have you wondered why almost every naturally-birthed child shows up on this side of the universe with a cry? They announce their entrance into this physical world with tears. I witnessed this personally during the birth of each of our three children.

At birth, every baby is shocked because they existed in a different realm before this, one which is very different from this physical reality on earth. For the rest of the child's life, the innermost cry from the depth of their heart is the desire to express this idea: *I am a spiritual being having a physical experience.* The divine side of a child refers to the idea that every child, and for that matter every individual, is released by God and carries the image, the nature and the DNA of the Creator. This is why human beings can pursue science and animals cannot.

In a way, what the child has been trying to articulate is: *I am not just my name, I am not an extension of my biological parents, I am not my environment or culture, but I am a spiritual being sent here to fulfil a specific assignment, to make a contribution to the beauty of creation, and to leave this world a better place for the human race.*

Every child wants their spirituality and humanity to be recognised, harnessed and developed. When these are harmonised, and merged together in the right balance, the child is able to live their highest, sunniest self, and manifest their full potential.

The mind of a child is wired for attention from parents (or carers), and to seek a sense of significance, which is a desire and a need shared by all human beings.

As a result, most of the disruptive, unhealthy and unacceptable behaviour displayed by any child is a cry for attention, love and connection with their parents or carers. In a sense, the child is shouting, 'Help! I don't know how to communicate this cry of my heart'.

Most children appear to be unable to cope with an attention deficit. Most children will rather look for any form of attention – be it shouting, reprimanding, scolding, or even being hit – than receive no attention at all.

Understanding the mindset of a child in this way allows parents to respond appropriately to whining, tantrums, and disruptive behaviour. It allows us to see the underlying meaning of the 'cry' – to seek attention, acceptance, connection, love, or a sense of significance.

The problem is that a very young child (less than 5 years old) may not know the right way to express and articulate what their 'cry' is for.

Parents have two choices in response to such a 'cry' for attention:

- Respond calmly with understanding of their need for connection.

- React with no understanding, which reinforces the unacceptable behaviour and makes it even worse.

To understand your child and ensure more cooperation in a range of areas, please refer to **'Psychological Strategies for Parenting'** in Chapter 5.

What is the purpose of parenting?

I cannot help but refer to a quote by Solomon, one of the wisest kings who ever lived, written in the biggest best-seller of all times:

> *'Train up a child in the way he should go, and when he is old he will not depart from it. Direct your children onto the right path, and when they are older, they will not leave it.'* [3]

The purpose of parenting is succinctly captured by this profound, yet simple, statement in the Bible, which is worth exploring further.

Firstly, the main purpose of parenting is to offer training, direction, and leadership to your child – to train them, direct them, lead them, and teach them good habits and values for effective living. Of course, this assumes that the parent has the capacity to train and direct. Unfortunately, as important and as difficult as the role of the parent is, it is one that many embark on without any form of training. Most parents are not adequately

---

[3] From Proverbs 22:6 (New King James Version, and New Living Translation), written by King Solomon.

prepared or equipped for the role.

Parents can only give what they have. It's impossible to offer what you do not have. As a result of this lack, most parents leave the training of their children entirely to schools. As good as an education system may be, children still need training and direction from their parents prior to starting school, and to complement what the education system provides.

For any form of training to be effective, it has to be structured, planned, and carried out intentionally and consistently, just like how medical students are trained.

But what do parents have to train their children in, or train their children for?

According to Solomon, that wise author, we should train our children in the way **they** should go. This is not the way we may wish or want for them, not the way we deem fit, not the way we prefer them to go, and not where society or the school system wants them to go.

Remember the child's deepest cry: I am not just a biological mass, but a being released from the spirit realm to provide an answer to a problem in our world.

Even if you do not believe in God as the source of all life (and I respect your view, whatever it might be), you may alternatively view life as science does: as energy which is just taking on a new or a different form on this physical realm. Most of the atheists I know personally take no issue with the existence of a transcendent energy, a superpower, or God. Rather, they have a problem with the way religion has portrayed this God as a Being who hates and kills the people he has created. Of course, this appears to be a complete misrepresentation of the merciful God who wants a loving relationship with the human beings in His kingdom. Religion may divide us, but our relationship with God always has, and always will, unite us.

When a child is born, that child is sent by God to fulfil a purpose on earth. Therefore, the role of the parent is to help the child discover this purpose they are designed for, and then help them train and develop so they can excel at it. When parents abdicate this important role, the school system may provide a general training, but the outcome can be unpredictable. It can still accidentally coincide with purpose – for example, when a grown-up student chooses a subject at college or university that resonates with them and which they have a passion for, with a view to using these skills to address a problem they have been born to solve.

The key when it comes to training a child is that the discovery of purpose should precede the training. This has huge implications for our education system. The training should equip each child to be their best, by becoming the person who is fully fit to fulfil the assignment they were sent here to complete. You can achieve no sense of fulfilment if you are trained for something you were not sent here to do. This may explain why many trained professionals hate Monday mornings, and are not happy with what they do. The missing link is likely to be that they are working outside of what they are shaped for.

How can we raise a child whose future is predictable?

According to Solomon, the only guarantee that a child, when they are older, will not depart from the direction and leadership we give them is if we:

- Help them discover the way they should go, their passion, their gift(s), their purpose, what is in their heart, what they are wired for.

- Train them in this divinely-inspired natural gift so that they can serve humanity in this way, and leave this world a better place.

A child raised in this way will be happy and fulfilled to have contributed to this world in their own unique way.

This is the most important purpose of parenting – to help your child find their purpose, to train and nurture your child into a full 'human being' instead of a just a biological mass. It is to help your child acknowledge their purpose, honour it, and do all it takes to excel in it, in order to bless the wider world.

In the words of one of my most highly-regarded mentors, Dr Sunday Adelaja (DSA), the primary goal of parenting is to build a strong character and a core value system[4] within a child, and the ultimate purpose of parenting is to form a child's full personality. This means a person who has developed the qualities (value system) that reflect on their thinking processes, behaviour, and their uniqueness, thereby encouraging them to live for a purpose greater than themselves, and to make this world a better place.

You will find more on this value system in Chapter 6: '**The Essential Values for Children.**'

What do the parenting experts say?

The emphasis on training and developing our children as the main purpose of parenting can be seen in all the best-sellers of the parenting genre. For example, Carole and Nadim Saad, in their Amazon best-seller book, state that:

'Our ultimate goal as parents should be to develop our children's self-responsibility, self-discipline, and emotional resilience as these are the key factors that allow our

---

[4] See DSA - Dr Sunday Adelaja's Online Resources, on www.youtube.com/sundayadelajaofficial and www.sundayadelajablog.com.

children to stand strong on their own feet.'[5]

These highly reputable co-authors stress the importance of teaching our children to stand on their own feet, and face challenges of adulthood.

In her famous book, *Calm Parents, Happy Kids, The Secrets of Stress-free Parenting*, Markham (2014)[6] uses slightly different words to echo the same purpose or responsibility of parents. According to her, the emphasis should be on coaching, not controlling, to support both the short-term and long-term development of the child into a more confident, self-disciplined and emotionally-intelligent person.

In the words of best-selling authors Adele Faber and Elaine Mazilish:

> *'... most of the books on child-rearing tell us that one of our most important goals as parents is to help our children separate from us, to help them become independent individuals who will one day be able to function on their own without us...'*[7]

From the perspective of Steve Biddulph[8], a parent acts as a coach, a caregiver and an ally to the child, so that the child

---

[5] From Carole and Nadim Saad (2015), *Kids Don't Come with a Manual: The Essential Guide to a Happy Family Life,* London, Best of Parenting Publishing: p 171.

[6] From Laura Markham (2014), *Calm Parents, Happy Kids, The Secrets of Stress-free Parenting*, London, Vermillion/Ebury Publishing.

[7] From Adele Faber and Elaine Mazilish (2013), *How to Talk so Kids Will Listen & Listen so Kids Will Talk*, London, Piccadilly Press: p 139.

[8] From Steve Biddulph (2013), *Raising Girls: Helping your daughter to grow wise, warm and strong*, London, Harper Thorsons: p 23.

makes the journey from being secured, through to learning to explore, relating to other people, and discovering themselves, and eventually taking charge of their life.

All the above parenting experts use different linguistic representations to emphasise parents' role in training, coaching, and supporting their children to become a full 'personality'. This, according to Dr Sunday Adelaja (DSA), is someone who has discovered who they truly are, their purpose, and how to live for the benefit of humanity.

Parenting can also be seen as an opportunity to help a child on their journey to realise and attain their 'self-actualisation', a phrase coined by the psychology guru, Abraham Maslow, in his attempt to explain what motivates people to want to work and achieve results.

To facilitate the discovery of your child's purpose and offer training, please refer to Chapter 6: '**The Essential Values for Children**.'

The essential need for love (dignity, respect and honour)

We all yearn for love and desire, and to be treated with dignity, respect and honour so that we feel significant. This is built into all of us, and is true regardless of age.

Every child has a natural need for love – to be loved and also to express love. This need is wired into their very nature, and they express this desire for love from the very first day they are born. Children are unable to function well if this innate need for love is not met by their parents or the environment they find themselves in.

Sometimes, parents are unable to articulate or express love to their children in a way that the children understand and can, therefore, receive. Children view the concept of love in many ways, including attention, affection, affirmation, and so on. These are as essential for children as water, food, clothing, and shelter are. Living without any of these needs is unthinkable. Attention, affection and affirmation are utterly priceless to children. Let us briefly explore each of them further.

Attention

A child spells 'love' as *'time'*. Love to a child is the time and undivided attention we offer to them. Paying full attention can be one of the greatest gifts a parent can give their children. Spending time listening to them sends the signal that they matter to us, and that they are important, significant and valuable. Does your child deserve your attention?

Affection

Affection is a parent's ability to make the child feel loved, by offering lots of hugs, appropriate touches, and kisses. Children need unlimited amounts of our affection every single day. When children grow up lacking in affection from their parents, carers or loved ones, they spend the rest of their lives begging for it from elsewhere.

Affirmation

Children also need to hear how much we love them unconditionally. By constantly telling them of our admiration for them and how much we cherish them, and repeating this many times a day, we meet their need to receive love through affirmation. Affirmation from a parent means a lot to a child, regardless of their age.

Affirmation becomes even more essential when your child begins to doubt their worth. Every child goes through a period in their life when they doubt themselves and ask questions, such as:

- 'Am I good enough?'

- 'Am I beautiful or handsome enough?'

- 'Is my face okay?'

- 'Is my height okay?'

- 'Do my parents really love me?'

Affirmation can help put their mind to rest, enabling them to accept themselves and believe that they are good enough, are accepted, and are loved, regardless of what other people say about them. There is more on how to effectively affirm your child in Chapter 5 under '**Strategy No 6: Using the power of praise**.'

Why is demonstrating love so important to your child?

Success in parenting depends on our ability to establish a connection with our children, part of a deep-seated social contract. When children feel our unconditional love and acceptance, knowing that we will always protect them and support them in a trusting and loving relationship, they will be willing to cooperate with us. The application of parenting principles and ideas are likely to be better received in this situation, making your child more receptive to what you have to say.

In other words, children are more likely to respond positively if a loving bond and connection is established.

Parents need to say 'I love you' to their children. This may not come naturally to some parents. However, as a parent, I'm sure you certainly do not want your children to say when you are gone, 'I knew my mum/dad loved me, but s/he never said it.'

Besides, parents not only have to *say* 'I love you', they have to also *show* it. Love should be expressed through your actions, in hugs, words, and attitudes.

Ask yourself with your child: if you have shown that you love them, have you said it? And if you have said that you love them, have you shown it? The two are not mutually exclusive.

Does it mean you are a weak parent if you say 'I love you' often to your child? No! Strong parents say this to their children, and it actually strengthens both their children and their connection with them. Parents can be both strong *and* loving.

This leads us to the matter of parenting styles, and which has proven to be the most effective.

A note on parenting styles

The simple answer is: it depends on your circumstances and what you are trying to achieve. Children, just like parents, are all different. A one-size-fits-all approach may not be the best recommendation for your particular situation.

Although the **authoritative style** – which offers love and support along with high expectations – is said to be the most effective in raising well-adjusted children[9], I am of the firm belief that balance is important. Just like in many other areas of life, we should strike the right balance between extremes: controlling and laissez-faire, authoritative and permissive, authoritarian and neglectful.

For example, if both parents are disciplinarians, their children will have no breathing space. On the other hand, if both parents adopt a neglectful style, their children are likely to become spoilt brats with no sense of responsibility or boundaries.

In our home, my wife Linda, who has her own unique style, tends to focus more on the physical and emotional needs of our children, including their food and how they look: hairstyle, clothes, shoes, and so on. I, on the other hand, tend to pay more attention to their studies, spirituality, and values, such as hard work, responsibility, and resilience. This translates into two quite different approaches. For example, Linda may want to provide everything the children want, while I often want them to wait for non-essentials, in order to teach them patience and delayed gratification.

With an understanding that we are working together as a team, and because we recognise that each of our approaches are important, we have found a great balance in meeting the physical, emotional, intellectual, and spiritual needs of our children.

Striking the right balance is the key to raising children to become their best.

---

[9] From Laura Markham (2014), *Calm Parents, Happy Kids, The Secrets of Stress-free Parenting*, London, Vermillion/Ebury Publishing: p 166

Activities for parents

Below are some activities you can try, to internalise this idea that one of the primary purposes of parenting is to respond to your child's essential need for love, dignity, respect and honour.

I want to intentionally tell my child, 'I love you' ……….. times a day for a period of ……. (this needs to be specific; e.g., a week, a month, etc.)

At the end of the period, check if you were on target, and the reaction of your child to this new approach.

How many instances did you say 'I love you' to your child?
- ……………………………………………………………………………………
……………………………………………………………………………………

What was your child's response?
- ……………………………………………………………………………………
………………………
- ……………………………………………………………………………………
………………………
- ……………………………………………………………………………………
………………………

I want to intentionally give ……….. hugs, appropriate or meaningful touches and kisses a day for ……….. (this needs to be specific; e.g., a week, a month, etc.)

At the end of the period, check if you were on target, and the reaction of your child to this new approach.

How many hugs, appropriate kisses/touches did you give your child?

- ....
  ....

What was your child's response?

- ....
  ....

- ....
  ....

- ....
  ....

I will intentionally plan a moment in the day where I listen to my child with full attention and assess the impact.

After a week or a month, check the reaction of your child to this new approach.

My child's response and the observed impact on our relationship:

- ....
  ....

- ....
  ....

- ....
  ....

It may initially feel awkward, but if you don't give up, the desired outcome (to intimately connect with your child) will be established.

Alternatively, you may use the goal-setting template below:

Goal-setting template

What do I want? (State the goal clearly, making it specific)	Why do I want this?	What can I do every day to move a step towards achieving the goal?	How and by when do I want to achieve this goal?

The fundamentals of parenting in a nutshell

- Every child has a deep innate need for a sense of love and significance.

- The deepest cry of the heart of every child is for both their divinity (higher self) and humanity (lower self) to be recognised, and to understand that regardless of their race, place and circumstance of birth, gender, physical attributes, and abilities or disabilities they are a being released from the spirit realm in answer to a particular problem facing humanity.

- Most of the disruptive or unhealthy behaviour displayed by children is a cry for attention, love and connection with their parents or carers. Parents can either respond calmly with understanding of this need, or react in a way which reinforces the unacceptable behaviour.

- Attention, affection and affirmation are essential for your child's wellbeing. Children who grow up without affection from their parents or carers spend the rest of their lives looking for it elsewhere.

- When children feel our unconditional love and acceptance, they are also more willing to cooperate with us.

- Parenting experts agree that we must teach our children to stand on their own feet, and face challenges of adulthood.

- The essential role of parenting is to help children to discover themselves, and their purpose, in an environment of love. Please refer to how to help your child discover their purpose in **Chapter 6: The Essential Values for Children,** under '**Purpose**'.

- Just like in many other areas of life, we should strike the right balance between extremes in our approach to parenting.

Notes

Chapter 3: Fundamental Strategies for Parenting

In this chapter, you will be introduced to:

- **Strategy No 1: Separate the "Who" from the "Do"**

  o Real life experience

  o How to separate a child's identity from their actions, so as to avoid labelling them

  o Activities for parents

- **Strategy No 2: Looking after yourself first**

  o What do we fill ourselves with?

  o Real life experience

  o Ideas for looking after yourself, so you can give to your child

  o Activities for parents

- **Strategy No 3: Leading by example**

  o Real life experience

  o Ideas for leading by being an example

  o Activities for parents

- The fundamental strategies for parenting in a nutshell

Strategy No 1: Separate the 'Who' from the 'Do'

This is a strategy to help address the action, and not the individual. It is another way to help build a loving relationship with your children – to learn to separate their actions from their personality. This allows you to deal separately with *what* they do or say, and *who* they are. Although what children *do* may not warrant our respect, who they *are* deserves dignity and respect, irrespective of what they do or how they behave.

Seeing a child in this perspective helps avoid perceiving your child as the problem or as an enemy. When actions are not separated from the person, we end up embarking on character assassination. I urge parents to be tough on unacceptable issues but soft on the child. Difficult moments should be revisited when there is calm, so that parents are better able to separate the issues from the child as a person.

> ***A typical child may be thinking:*** *'but I am a good person who happened to have done something bad, I don't understand why my parents are so mad at me. Don't they make mistakes in life?'*

Your child, just like any other human being, is an offspring of the Creator, and shares the image and identity of God. By virtue of this, they deserve love, respect, and dignity, regardless of their actions. Any attack, accusation, anger, or insult should never have to be directed at the person. For example, avoid statements like:

> *'You are lazy.'*
> *'You are stupid.'*
> *'You are careless.'*
> *'You are useless.'*

These are all a direct attack on the child's identity, or the **'Who'**.

There are a number of problems with this attitude towards our children. Firstly, we insult the Creator and the divine in the child.

Secondly, to the child, these statements are perceived as blaming, accusation, name-calling, and insults, and may actually define who they are, particularly of they hear it repeated over and over again, over a long time. This makes them conclude, 'This is who I am: I am lazy, I am incapable.' And this only reinforces their behaviour.

Thirdly, the natural response to statements like these is that of defence, resentment, anger, and retaliation, causing the bond between the child and the parent to be broken.

Besides these reasons, the bigger problem with this approach, which most parents adopt unconsciously, is that it fails to address the **'Do'**, or the action by the child which needs correction.

Parents should never place negative labels on their children, like the ones we have looked at above. These labels become self-fulfilling, by just thinking them in our minds long enough. Rather, we should address the real issues – that is, 'Your behaviour was unacceptable', or 'What you said was unkind', and so on.

According to the research, 80% of our interactions with our children are made up of negative statements and comments. These come across to the child as a direct criticism or insult, or as an attempt to blame or to disrespect them. Mostly, these unhelpful actions are not made consciously by parents.[10]

---

[10] From Carole and Nadim Saad (2015), *Kids Don't Come with a Manual: The Essential Guide to a Happy Family Life,* London, Best of Parenting Publishing: p 130.

Parents engage impulsively in this way with their children as an automatic approach to parenting. The problem is that these negative comments are mainly in the form of a personal attack on the child's 'Who', and completely fails to address the 'Do', the action that needs correction.

Imagine what the outcome would be if you are able to switch around this ratio of 80% negative to 20% positive comments. 80% of your interactions with your children could be positive and appreciative, encouraging and praising, and only 20% negative.

Another way to avoid attacking your child's personality with negative 'You are...' statements is for parents to talk about their feelings by replacing 'You' with 'I'. For example, 'You are troublesome' can instead be expressed as 'I feel disturbed or worried when I see.... or hear.... this action in the house.'

The following are a few ways to rephrase unhelpful statements so that they address the issue at hand rather than attack the child, which tends to be counterproductive:

- 'You are lazy!' can be rephrased as, 'That action did not show hard work.'

- 'You are callous!' can become, 'That remark was unkind.'

- 'You are disgraceful!' can become, 'That action made me feel uncomfortable.'

- 'You are disrespectful!' can become, 'I am not impressed with what I am hearing or seeing. I expect my love and kindness to be reciprocated.'

- 'You are troublesome' can become, 'That action drains me of all my energy, and I know you don't want to leave your mum/dad with no energy. Do you?'

Real life experience

It was getting dark. The children had come back from school, and they were playing together in the house. In came the youngest child (she has asked to be called 'Elizabeth' in this book), who was only six at the time. She was crying about something her sister ('Kylie') had said.

'Dad, Kylie said I am stupid.'

I acknowledged her feelings by saying, 'That must hurt.'

'Yeah,' she replied.

I would normally let them solve their own problems, but this time I wanted to highlight a fundamental lesson. So I asked, 'What did you do to make Kylie call you names?'

'I didn't do anything!' she replied.

I called Kylie in and asked for her version of the incident.

'What happened, Kylie?'

'Elizabeth was not arranging my game properly and that made me angry.'

'So did you say she is stupid?' I asked.

'No! I meant what she was doing was not clever,' said Kylie.

I was so glad to see that my eldest daughter had absorbed the idea of separating a person's 'Do' from their 'Who', even at her age.

'Elizabeth,' I said. 'You are a good person who happens to have done something not so clever. You are not a stupid person. Kylie was only referring to your action, what you did, and not who you are. So, are you stupid?'

'No,' she replied, laughing.

When we separate children's actions from their personality, and address their actions while still showing love and respect for their identity, then they feel better and we feel better. And, ultimately, this creates a happy home.

How to separate a child's identity from their

actions, so as to avoid labelling them

1. Do not begin a negative comment with 'you'. It makes the statement sound like a direct attack on the identity and character of the child.

2. Instead, describe the problem. For example, 'I can see the room is messy', rather than 'You are a lazy boy, you cannot even keep your room tidy.' In this way, the focus is shifted to the problem that needs solving, and the child is better able to cooperate and deal with the problem themselves. Accusations and personal attacks never get the work done, it only makes your child feel angry, disrespected, and defensive.

3. Replace the word 'you' with 'I' in negative situations, so that you describe your feelings without attacking the child. For example, 'I feel disrespected when I am talked to that way', instead of, 'You insulted me, you are shameful.'

Activities for parents

Below are some activities you can try, to internalise this idea that you can separate a child's identity from their actions so as to avoid labelling them.

When I get triggered by my child's behaviour, I usually, but unintentionally, express it as follows:

- 'You are

  ....,
  ....'

- 'You are

  ....,
  ....'

- By swearing: Yes/no

- By shouting: Yes/no

The new approach I want to explore is to consciously set goal(s) to only describe the problem in the heat of the moment when I feel triggered. For example – for the coming week, when I am upset with my child, I will not shout at them, or I will remain calm and describe the unacceptable behaviour without using 'you'...

- Goal #1

  ....

- Goal #2

  ....

- Goal #3

  ....

Review after one week, and again after one month. How did my child's behaviour change in response to the new approach?

- ....
  ....

- ....
  ....

- ....
  ....

This takes time and effort, so be patient. Keep on trying new ways of just describing what you see, until it becomes second nature and begins to work for you. Alternatively, you may use the goal-setting template below:

Goal-setting template

What do I want? (State the goal clearly, making it specific)	Why do I want this?	What can I do every day to move a step towards achieving the goal?	How and by when do I want to achieve this goal?

Strategy No 2: Looking after yourself first

This strategy emphasises the importance of self-care. A major problem with parenting is the difficulty involved when a parent tries to give what they do not have. It is just not possible to do this. That is why it is vitally important to fill yourself up first, so that you are able to give naturally and effortlessly from that source. This allows us to give our best to our children, and not the leftovers of ourselves. Our parenting will emanate from a place of love rather than coming out of fear or worry.

> *A typical child may be thinking:* '*I don't get it, why are my parents always arguing? It makes me feel anxious and uneasy. If they cannot manage or harness their emotions, how do they expect me to?*'

What do we fill ourselves with?

We can fill ourselves with joy, by acknowledging the joy already inside of us.

For example, we can find something we have or something around us in each present moment and be grateful for it. Focusing on the positive enables us to significantly change our emotional state and feelings. For example, by noticing how blessed we are to have been entrusted with a child and appreciating this fact can trigger joy inside of us. Not all adults are able to have children.

The UK's National Health Service (NHS) puts the number of couples having difficulty conceiving at about 3.5 million, that is, approximately 1 in every 7 couples in the UK.[11] It is a privilege and an honour, and one which comes with a huge responsibility, like many other privileges in life.

One can always find something to savour, appreciate, and be grateful for. If you are still breathing and have the strength to get up today, appreciate it and be grateful for it, as not all people are this lucky.

Remember that it is almost impossible to achieve a state of perfection on this side of eternity. No one has 100% of everything working for them all of the time. One of the secrets of happiness is our ability to be selective about what we choose to focus on. If we find just one positive thing to be grateful for, it changes our unhappy feelings to brighter ones. By doing this, we fill ourselves and we are able to give to our children from the overflow, rather than trying to operate from an empty tank.

We can also fill ourselves with the right information. Light comes from knowledge – knowledge about yourself, your child, and your relationship with your child. It starts and ends with us as parents. Developing and looking after yourself in this way first, helps prevent you being easily triggered by your children's actions and other events.

Real life experience

In the story I shared in Chapter 1, I needed to take some time off to sort myself out. I spent days deeply reflecting on and processing what had happened. I was experiencing some very negative feelings, but I had to get myself out of that place and find my way to a place of peace and love. Only there could I

---

[11] From the website of the UK's National Health Service (NHS): https://www.nhs.uk/conditions/infertility.

begin to see the positive lessons I could take away from what had unfolded.

We all have moments like that. Have you experienced a period of your life when everything seemed so low, you believed you were at the lowest point in your whole life?

Ideas for looking after yourself, so you can give to your child

- Solitude: spend some time alone to recharge your batteries. Give yourself some 'me time.'

- In solitude, it is recommended to practice mindful breathing or meditation by following these simple steps:

    o Sit down and close your eyes.

    o Take a deep breath through your nose, hold it, then inhale again to fill your whole diaphragm or lungs or stomach (5-10 seconds), before breathing out slowly but evenly through your mouth (5-10 seconds).

    o Repeat this process of breathing in and out while focusing your mind on your breath, and try to just be in the present moment for 3 -10 minutes.

    o Make this a habitual practice, two to three times a day, preferably including first thing in the morning and last thing before sleep at night.

    o Any time you find yourself experiencing anxiety, worry, fear, anger, or other difficult or negative emotions, give yourself a few minutes to breathe deeply in and out. This should help to restore you to a peaceful state. Check how you feel after each mindful breathing session. A child can be taught this practice from the age of five, and it is a very useful life skill to share.

- Right after the above meditation is a good time to think, review or reflect on your actions, and ask questions to guide the way forward, such as:

  o What did I do right?

  o How can I make it even better the next time around?

- Continuously learn from other parents, particularly those who have gone through tough times and have success stories to share, through their books, online videos, mentorship or coaching.

- Take up activities to help you relax: visiting friends, for example, or a night out with your partner, or sports or video games.

- Appreciate yourself. Find two things you can appreciate about yourself; for example, you were not selfish, you didn't raise your voice even when provoked, you were able to manage your emotions.

- Allow yourself to accept and love yourself. Speak love to yourself (your internal dialogue), which is the conversation that matters most.

- Don't blame yourself: when it comes to parenting, perfection is unattainable and non-existent. Just try your best to pursue continuous, ongoing improvement.

Activities for parents

Below are some activities you can try, to internalise this strategy of looking after yourself.

Set a goal or goals to free up time or set a specific time aside for yourself daily to do mindful breathing and to learn more about yourself and your child:

- Goal #1
  ....

- Goal #2
  ....

- Goal #3
  ....

Review: How did my child's behaviour change in response to the new approach?

- ....
  ....

- ....
  ....

- ....
  ....

This takes time and effort, so be patient. Keep on trying, as this inner strength will pay off in many aspects of your life, including by building a good relationship with your child. Alternatively, you may use the goal-setting template below:

Goal-setting template

What do I want? (State the goal clearly, making it specific)	Why do I want this?	What can I do every day to move a step towards achieving the goal?	How and by when do I want to achieve this goal?

Strategy No 3: Leading by example

This strategy is about modelling good behaviour for our children. Parenting is a challenging leadership role which requires knowledge, understanding, wisdom, and a specialised skillset if you are to play it well. Children need our leadership. They want to see us demonstrate what we tell them and expect them to do. This is called **modelling**.

> *A typical child may be thinking:* 'Why do my parents want me to do something they themselves don't want to do? Why do they shout at me, but accuse me of being rude when I raise my voice? This is hypocrisy and grossly unfair.'

We can show our children how to behave through carefully choosing our words, how we say them, and our actions. This gives them the opportunity to easily observe and copy us, which will happen almost automatically.

The modelling role played by parents is vitally crucial for every child, as parents can be the most influential teachers in a child's life, right through until adulthood. Children don't only need to **hear** what we want them to do – they need to **see** what we expect from them modelled and demonstrated to them in an intentional way.

For example, if parents want respect and responsible behaviour from a child, they have to lead the way from a place of dignity and respect so that the child can be expected to respond accordingly.

On the other hand, when we as parents lead from a place of fear, hurt and hatred, seeing our child as an enemy, and demonstrating this by shouting most of the time, we can expect the child to mirror this back to us by screaming at us. I get very surprised when I'm picking my children up from school and hear other kids shout at their parents: 'I hate you!' It makes me think that something is fundamentally wrong. Those children may have had this kind of behaviour modelled to them. When something like this is repeated, the subconscious can accept it as the norm and even as a command.

Leading by example requires parents to be equipped with the right tools. Again, parents cannot give what they do not have. When parents are inadequately prepared for this leadership role, we tend to hear interactions like this:

'Do what I say and not what I do!'

This parenting strategy is ineffective and inauthentic. Your child will spot the hypocrisy and this in turn will undermine your authority as a parent.

Simply put, parenting starts with the parent. As a parent, are you ready to lead? Do you want to become a role model for your child? If we want our children to be calm, we have to learn to harness our own emotions and remain calm when our buttons are pushed, such that the natural response is to scream at our children.

Real life experience

Our first-born, Andrea (as she has asked to be called here) hated her secondary school when she first started attending it. This was mainly because she had to get up very early in the morning to get ready and catch the bus for a 30-minute commute. Before that, she used to only spend 5 minutes walking to her primary school, so this change was a huge shock for her. I acknowledged her feelings but also had to model and be an example to her. So what did I do? I changed my sleeping and work patterns to get up even earlier than she had to.

One morning, she was miserably unhappy. 'I hate this school,' she moaned.

'Yes, I know how hard it is to have to get up early in the morning when most people are still sleeping,' I whispered. 'I know this because I had to struggle to get up to study myself, but the moment I take a shower or wash my face, the feeling disappears.'

This has worked very well, as by the time she is up she sees me already in my study. Modelling what we want our children to do is a very effective way of getting the message across in parenting.

Ideas for leading by being an example

- Show unconditional love and acceptance towards your child at all times. This is easy to say but hard to do. We should aim to show love for and accept our children when they need it most – that is, when they do not deserve it.

- Do not shout at your child, regardless of their actions, unless there is an emergency. Instead, pause, take in a deep breath, and leave the room if possible, or say 'I cannot talk now...' This is the best option, because expressing anger in the heat of the moment can make us even angrier and this infects our children as well.

- Practise joy and gratitude, and replenish your spirit, so you are able to give your best to others in turn. Please refer to **Strategy No. 2: Looking after yourself first**, where I speak about how to practise mindfulness.

Activities for parents

Below are some activities you can try, to internalise this strategy of leading by example.

Set goals not to shout at your child for a whole day, regardless of what they do, and to respect them. For example, 'I will remain calm by pausing and taking deep breaths, and keep my cool for the next .... minutes/hours', or 'I will model love, dignity and respect to my child for the next .... minutes/hours.'

- Goal #1

  ....

- Goal #2

  ....

- Goal #3

  ....

Review after one week, and again after one month. How did my child's behaviour change?

- ....
  ....

- ....
  ....

- ....
  ....

This takes time and effort, so be patient. Keep on trying, as this inner strength will pay off in many aspects of your life, including by building a good relationship with your child. Alternatively, you may use the goal-setting template below:

Goal-setting template

What do I want? (State the goal clearly, making it specific)	Why do I want this?	What can I do every day to move a step towards achieving the goal?	How and by when do I want to achieve this goal?

Fundamental strategies for parenting in a nutshell

- Parents are advised to separate a child's identity (their '**Who**') from their actions (their '**Do**'). Be soft and loving on the child but firm on unacceptable actions.

- You should address issues and problematic behaviour without coming across as blaming, accusing, attacking, or labelling the child as a person.

- Parents are encouraged to nurture themselves first, so that they are in a position to give the best of themselves, not what is left of themselves.

- Children want to see how to manage life, by having good behaviours modelled for them by their parents.

- We can show our children how to behave through carefully choosing our words and our actions.

Notes

Chapter 4: The Psychological Side of Children

In this chapter, you will be introduced to:

- The fuel metaphor

- Psychology versus spirituality

- How do we hurt our children's feelings and emotions, and end up discouraging them?

- Ideas for building and maintaining positive emotions and feelings in your child

- What is wrong with punishment as a method of discipline?

- What about shouting?

- What about time out?

- Real life experience

- Ideas for moving towards more effective forms of discipline

- Activities for parents

- Goal setting template

- The Psychological side of children in the nutshell

The fuel metaphor

As I was reflecting on psychology, which has got to do with the mind, emotions, and feelings and their tremendously influential impact on children, I was reminded of the driving experience of a friend.

This guy had an unforgettable experience while driving on the M25 surrounding Greater London. He saw the fuel warning light come on, but he thought he could manage the remaining miles to the next service station. After a few minutes, the car ran out of fuel, and came to a stop. It wouldn't move again. He was stuck in no-man's land. He eventually got assistance to the nearest service station. He was so frustrated that he ended up filling the tank up completely.

He got back on the road, but after a few minutes the car stopped abruptly and the engine would not start again. 'What's wrong now?!' he shouted. He got mad at the car and upset at everyone, including himself. He had to call for roadside assistance again. On inspection, the mechanic realised the wrong fuel has been put in the car. Instead of diesel, the car had been filled up with petrol, which had now damaged the fuel pump and engine. Guess what happened next?

As fuel is to the functioning of a car, so are emotions and feelings to the functioning of a human being. Emotions or feelings are what drive our productivity.

A car will not work without fuel. Similarly, children, or human beings in general, are unable to work effectively if there is no fuel, or the wrong fuel (that is, bad feelings). When you put the wrong fuel in a car, what happens? It won't work, of course, and will even get damaged. This is the equivalent of upsetting children or people, and making them feel bad. It causes emotional damage, wounds and scars, just like dents on damaged cars.

Am I saying that parents should condone the unacceptable behaviour of their children? No! Parents should not sweep issues under the carpet, but try to see the cause of the behaviour from the child's perspective. Difficult behaviour in children is usually a cry for help, for attention, or for acceptance. As a result, the focus should be on the relationship as needing work or repair.

The repair needed as a result of the wounds caused by words is costly and time-consuming. So, a mastery of **emotional intelligence** or EQ is one of the single most important skills every parent must master to get along well with their children. Please refer to **Strategy No 4: Letting your child feel heard and listened to**, in Chapter 5, for more about EQ.

Psychology versus spirituality

Humans are tripartite beings, or three-part beings, who have a spirit, a soul, and a body. The divine aspect of humans, the life-giving part, is the spirit, which contains the 'DNA' of the Creator.[12] I see spirituality as having a personal relationship or an inward connection, by faith, with an unseen 'Father', or God, and becoming aware of the infinite wisdom and capabilities that flow from this intimate relationship, allowing us to perceive reality beyond the limitations of the five human senses.

Psychology, or the study of the human mind and how it controls our behaviour, recognises the more human aspect of us all. It places emphasis on the soul, which is the mental and the emotional part of human beings.

The vitally important psychological dimension of every child has to do with the soul, which consists of the child's emotions,

---

[12] From Andrew Wommack (2016), *Spirit, Soul & Body*, New Edition, Glasgow, Bell & Bain.

feelings, the mind/brain, the will, the mental state, and their personality, which drive their behaviour and appear to be the most important part determining their effectiveness on earth.

This may explain why the school system encourages the development of mental abilities, through compulsory education for up to 16- or 18-year-olds, in many countries.

As a parent, learning to harness your own feelings and helping your child manage theirs is crucial for their wellbeing. Parents have a leading role to play, particularly when children are very young (0-3 years) and do not know how to express their feelings in a better, more positive way. Parents can either facilitate their child's ability to express emotions positively, or make the situation worse by hurting their child's feelings with an ill-judged word or action. Hurt, when allowed to build up and fester, has a detrimental effect on the mental wellbeing of our children.

The huge importance of the psychological side of a child's development reminds me of a famous quote by Paul, one of the most highly educated and influential apostles of his era: *'Fathers, do not provoke your children, lest they become discouraged.'*[13]

Children become discouraged and unable to cooperate when they are disheartened, or their emotions and feelings are badly hurt. Child psychology, with its focus on the mind, emotions, and feelings of the child, has a crucial role to play in helping parents to encourage their children and not leave them discouraged, emotionally injured, or wounded. As a result, this next section is informed by the lessons and ideas from the field of psychology.

---

[13] From Colossians 3:21 (New King James Version), written by Apostle Paul.

How do we hurt our children's feelings and emotions, and end up discouraging them?

Knowingly or unknowingly, intentionally or unintentionally, we frequently cause deep wounds and injuries in the souls of our children, the seat of their feelings and emotions. We do this through careless words and actions that do not show love, compassion and care.

Inconsiderate words can hurt. It is easy to remember the unkind words spoken to us by parents, teachers, friends, and those we least expected to hear them from. Can you recall the feeling those words generated inside of you, and how your mood was affected? It is the same with your children. Our words, particularly negative ones spoken without care or in anger, have the potential to leave indelible wounds in a child's psyche.

When we create good feelings in our children through our words and actions, they are naturally motivated to want to listen, learn, and cooperate. On the other hand, when they are heartbroken and discouraged, they are unable to hear or take instructions and guidance from us.

This is why Paul's statement above – instructing parents to never, ever attempt to provoke their children – can be seen to have a deep psychological significance. There is so much wisdom in this statement, which can be understood as a command to all parents who want to encourage cooperation from their children. This makes absolute sense, as children's behaviour is significantly influenced by their emotional state. Although this is applicable to all children, and even adults, it is particularly important and true for children below the age of three, as they have less capacity to process what they hear and see from their parents.

Let's face it: the average person does not like to be criticised in any way, shape, or form. Have you met anyone who likes receiving criticism and loves to be corrected? Our instinctive feelings perceive criticism as an attack on our pride, and it cuts straight to our fears, our immaturity as a result of deep wounds, or the broken places in us that need healing. It fires up the defensive forces within us.

This natural 'allergy' to criticism is true for children as well. It takes a mature and a secure individual to be comfortable with criticism and actually embrace it. This is a capacity most young people may not have yet developed.

Dr Laura Markham[14] includes in her book a famous study about toddlers' ability to control themselves in order to achieve a goal. First, children were asked if they wanted one biscuit or two, and all of them expressed a desire for two. The children were then given a test – one biscuit was given to each child and the researcher gave them the choice to either eat it, or wait while he left the room for a few minutes. Those who were able to wait and not eat the biscuit, he explained, would receive an additional biscuit to eat on his return.

What do you think happened? The research shows that not a single toddler was able to control their impulse and wait. At that young age (0-3), children have not developed the capacity to control their impulses, emotions, and feelings. The study shows that when the children are of pre-school age (3-5 years), about 30% of them are able to control their impulses and wait to get the second biscuit.

This has enormous implications for parenting. When children throw tantrums and act irrationally, parents are to show understanding, provide support, education, and encouragement to help them harness their emotions.

---

[14] From Laura Markham (2014), *Calm Parents, Happy Kids, The Secrets of Stress-free Parenting*, London, Vermillion/Ebury Publishing: p 216.

Ideas for building and maintaining positive emotions and feelings in your child

- *Choose your words carefully.* It is a good idea to pause and decide carefully how to articulate the ideas and information we want to pass on to our children, so that we come across as encouraging as possible.

- *Do not shout or raise your voice.* Research by body language experts suggests that about 38% of communication is made up by our tone of voice and how we say the words. The words themselves only account for 7%, and the remaining 55%[15] is down to our body language, such as non-verbal signals, posture and gestures. The lesson from this evidence is that the attitude, the tone and the volume with which we speak to our children matter as much as the words we use. How we say our words are more important than the literal meaning or the words. So speak with a soft, empathic, and loving tone of voice, free from anger. The only exception is when there is an emergency.

- *Apologise for your mistakes*. When we get it wrong, or find ourselves occasionally reverting to our old ways of doing things, we should be willing to apologise to our children and model this example to them. We teach them how we are all struggling and no one is perfect.

---

[15] From the Body Language Expert website, 'Communication - What Percentage is Body Language?', http://www.bodylanguageexpert.co.uk/communication-what-percentage-body-language.html.

What is wrong with punishment as a method of discipline?

Discipline, which is to guide or to coach, is not the same as punishment, which is '...*an action with an intent to hurt, either physically or psychologically, in order to teach a lesson.*'[16] The use of physical punishment is rife in many homes. Many parents use this form of discipline on their children, which includes smacking, spanking, slapping, beating, or striking with an object.

Pope Francis, the current and 266th Pope of the Catholic Church, was reported in 2015 by the UK's *Guardian Newspaper* to have said that smacking is fine in disciplining a child once their 'dignity is maintained'. He appeared to have made this statement in good faith, and did not mean to condone spanking that has elements of cruelty and violence. He meant only smacking meant to help with disciplining, correcting, guiding, instructing, and educating the child. However, this statement attracted huge criticism from many countries where smacking is illegal.

The UK's Children Act 2004, Section 58, states that it is illegal to smack a child. The exception to this rule is if the smacking amounts to 'reasonable punishment' or 'reasonable chastisement'. That is, if the smacking does not reflect child cruelty and is done with no intention to cause grievous bodily harm, or to leave bruises or marks on the body of the child.

In October 2017, it was reported in the UK's major newspapers that Scotland was the first country in the UK to ban

---

[16] From Laura Markham (2014), *Calm Parents, Happy Kids, The Secrets of Stress-free Parenting*, London, Vermillion/Ebury Publishing: p 149.

smacking completely. *The Guardian* actually called for a UK-wide ban to remove the legal defence of 'reasonable punishment' (which the Scots called 'justifiable assault' on a child, and found it unacceptable). This was to bring the UK in line with almost 50 countries – including Denmark, France, Germany, Ireland, Norway, and Sweden – which have placed a ban on smacking or any physical form of punishment for children, in compliance with the **United Nations Convention on the rights of the child (UNCRC),**

According to the statistics, 85% (that is, more than 4 in every 5) of adolescents surveyed in the United States admitted to having been slapped or smacked by their parents at some point in their lives.[17] The experts in child psychology, having been informed by recent research, unanimously agree that all forms of physical punishment are in fact counterproductive.

The above forms of physical punishment are ineffective ways to positively influence children for a number of reasons:

- They create a feeling of hatred in children of all ages towards their parents, which undermines the loving bond, the very basis of our relationship with them.

- They also leave children feeling unworthy, resentful, and guilty, and even cause them to plan revenge or arm themselves in some way, shape or form against us.

- They take the focus away from the main issue, and fail to address the problem at stake, therefore depriving the child the opportunity to face their wrongdoings and take responsibility or make amends.

---

[17] From Laura Markham (2014), *Calm Parents, Happy Kids, The Secrets of Stress-free Parenting*, London, Vermillion/Ebury Publishing: p 170.

At this point, you may be asking:

1. So, is there no benefit from physical punishment?

2. Without punishment, won't I be losing my last means of control as a parent and putting my child in charge?

3. What about the statement 'spare the rod, spoil the child'?

Let us address each of these questions in turn.

1) So, is there any benefit from physical punishment?

Psychologist and parenting expert Dr Laura Markham has brilliantly summarised the 60 years of research that exists on corporal and harsh physical discipline done, carried out by Dr Elizabeth Gershoff.

Gershoff *'found that the only positive outcome of corporal punishment was immediate compliance'* but that it ensured less long-term compliance and came with many negative effects, such as increased aggression, mental health problems, relationship problems with parents and others, and sibling violence, and concluded that *'smacking damages kids' psyches and worsens behaviour'*.[18]

However, in January 2010, the UK's *Daily Mail* and *Daily Telegraph* newspapers reported evidence from a study in the United States which suggests that children who are smacked up to the age of 6 by their parents may do better at school and grow up to be happier and more successful in life than those

---

[18] From Laura Markham (2014), *Calm Parents, Happy Kids, The Secrets of Stress-free Parenting*, London, Vermillion/Ebury Publishing: p 171.

who were spared physical discipline, and therefore recommended that parents should not be criminalised for reasonable smacking or chastisement. But the study also revealed that teenagers that are still continuously spanked performed worst across all the categories.[19]

2) Without punishment, won't I be losing my last means of control and putting my child in charge?

A parenting environment without physical punishment does not strip a parent of their control. On the contrary, it actually empowers parents to guide and coach rather than to try to control their children.

This punishment-free approach allows children to face the consequences of their misbehaviour, so that they can take responsibility for their actions and learn crucial life lessons from the experience. This approach has long-term positive effects. Punishment takes this opportunity away from children.

3) What about the statement 'spare the rod, spoil the child'?

This question is inspired by the following statement: *'Those who spare the rod of discipline hate their children. Those who love their children care enough to discipline them.'*[20] The 'rod' can be seen as a shepherd's staff, to help provide loving care, guidance, and correction. This quotation means that a failure to

---

[19] See articles http://www.dailymail.co.uk/news/article-1240279/Children-smacked-young-likely-successful-study-finds.html and http://www.telegraph.co.uk/news/health/news/6926823/Smacked-children-more-successful-later-in-life-study-finds.html.

[20] From Proverbs 13:24 (New Living Translation), written by King Solomon.

discipline and guide a child is an act of hatred towards that child, as they may grow up without boundaries and respect for law, order, people, or property, which they may eventually learn the hard way in a prison.

However, I strongly believe that 'discipline' in this context does not mean physical punishment intended to hurt in order to correct the child, despite what the rod metaphor seems to suggest. Although I am not completely against corporal punishment, I am wholeheartedly in favour of discipline, not abuse.

Just think about this – when a child smacks another child, it is called aggression, and seen as unacceptable. When a child hits an adult, it is called hostility. When an adult hits another adult, it is called an assault, which is unlawful physical attack punishable by law. But when an adult hits or spanks a child we want to call it discipline? Seriously? This sounds more like abuse. What do you think?

Children can be allowed to face the natural consequences of their actions without being subjected to physical punishment. This is what the Creator modelled for the human race, according to the story in the Garden of Eden, prior to the introduction of written laws. When Adam and Eve rebelled, their Heavenly Father allowed them to face the natural consequences of what He had already warned them of, but He did not withdraw His love for them.

This revealed and continues to reveal an alternative to physical punishment. Parents should be firm, but let their children experience the natural consequences of their actions and choices instead of resorting to smacking or any form of physical punishment, which apart from being counterproductive, has many adverse effects on the child based on the research in this field.

Let me put this 'rod' metaphor in the Bible in the broader context of the Kingdom of God. According to the Biblical account, the written law was introduced about 2,500 years after the separation of the first 'children' from God, along with the associated punishment for non-compliance. The Old Testament laws were never intended as a means of justification. The following are some of the intended purposes of the laws:

- To continue the fundamental principle allowing human beings to exercise their free will and freedom of choice.

- To establish standards, and bring order and boundaries to life.

- To reveal how terrible sin is.

- To make people fearful in order to restrain sin, so as to keep the plan of salvation on track.

- To show mankind how it is almost impossible to keep the written laws as a means of justification or acceptance with God using our human efforts (as no one could in that era).

- And, more importantly, to help mankind to realise their need for a Saviour.

Although the Old Testament laws were and are good at achieving the above purposes, they appear to have done a tremendous damage by completely misrepresenting God as a merciless, unforgiving, angry, controlling, difficult to please, vindictive, and bloodthirsty Being.

The good news for the human race is that we are presented with the same choice as Adam and Eve had before the written law came, to relate to God as a loving Father one more time. In this dispensation, the Father provides loving correction by first showing mercy and empathy for those who accept His love. The only sin that sends people to hell is the rejection of the sacrifice it took to restore the relationship.[21] God's judgement is not meant for human beings, but the devil and those who willingly choose to follow him.

What has this got to do with parenting?

Some parents realise that when they are able to receive this unconditional love and acceptance from the Heavenly Father, they obtain the capacity to be able to easily extend the same to their children. In my story in Chapter 1, I discovered that we as parents can also misrepresent God's nature to our children when we resort to punishment as a means of discipline. When I used corporal punishment, I earned no bond or loving relationship with my children.

It was when I began to parent from a place of unconditional love that my children could connect with me, and more easily relate to God as a Father. I was reduced to tears of joy when I received the following letter from one of my daughters on my latest birthday:

> Dear Dad,
> I want to start off by saying happy birthday. I hope you achieve great things this year. You're not just my dad, you're my best friend. You're someone I can say thank you to and one of the most understanding people I know (not to mention a great listener). You deserve so much. You could get the best dad of the year award and I wouldn't be surprised. You have taught me so much and

---

[21] From John 6:47, John 8:4-11, and John 16:8-11 (New King James Version, and New Living Translation), written by Apostle John.

I wouldn't be who I am without you. I hope your wishes come true but I already know that you will succeed. I believe in you. You truly are the best dad in the world. I am definitely the luckiest daughter. I will never forget you and you will always be in my heart until the day I die. You may think I am just writing this down and don't mean it but every word is from the bottom of my heart. I wish I could be like you. I wish people could look at me the way they look at you. Resilient, kind, loving, understanding, funny at times, and most of all an example of what God wants people to live like. I love you daddy. Always have, always will

From Princess
Your lucky daughter

What about shouting?

The definition of punishment is the intention to cause physical or psychological hurt in an attempt to teach a lesson. Shouting is an emotionally painful punishment. It communicates no respect or dignity for the child, and comes from a place of fear and anger instead of a place of unconditional love. Losing one's temper and operating from anger pushes children away from the connection we have with them (for more on this, please refer to **Strategy No 1: Separate the 'Who' from the 'Do'**).

Also, shouting at a child shows them that this way of expressing emotions is normal and acceptable. Within no time at all, we are likely to find them shouting back at us. Young children in particular have little or no capacity to process what they see and hear. For example, some young children find themselves shouting 'I hate you' at their parents, just because they have heard someone else say that sentence and they find it 'cool' to copy others and throw that devastatingly painful sentence at their own parents. It is, therefore, important that parents show the way by being an example and a role model for their children.

What about time out?

According to Wikipedia[21], 'time-out' or social exclusion is:

> '... a form of behavioral modification that involves temporarily separating a person from an environment where unacceptable behavior has occurred. The goal is to remove that person from an enriched, enjoyable environment, and therefore lead to extinction of the offending behavior. It is an educational and parenting technique recommended by most pediatricians and developmental psychologists as an effective form of discipline. Often a corner (hence the common term corner time) or a similar space where the person is to stand or sit during time-outs is designated. This form of discipline is especially popular in western cultures.'[22]

Although using a time-out is far better than physical punishment, and more humane than spanking, it is not optimally effective. This is because it fails to address the underlying problem, the root cause of what is making the child do those 'unacceptable' actions.

The intended aim of a time-out is to give the child an opportunity to reflect on what they have done, learn lessons, and come up with answers. But a typical child may already be feeling bad and this confinement may increase their feelings of guilt, shame, or pity, and simple reinforce the behaviour. Besides, children may perceive the time-out as a punishment, and their natural response is more likely to be resentful and

---

[22] See https://en.wikipedia.org/wiki/Time-out_(parenting).

planning a revenge.

The recommendation by parenting experts is **'time-in'**, a private time with the child to acknowledge their feelings and help them come up with better ways to express those difficult feelings, so that they do not hurt the feelings of others.

Real life experience

I was busy teaching a group of children how to play the musical keyboard free of charge. Kylie, one of my daughters, had decided to join me help them with the right fingering techniques. But she could not wait for her turn, and she started moving about, causing distractions. I offered her a choice:

'Do you want to stay here by sitting down quietly and help me teach them, or go out and play with the other children? You choose one.'

I continued, but no sooner had I restarted than Kylie resumed her distractive activities.

I stopped, hugged her and said, 'I am so sorry to let you go, but since you couldn't choose, I will help you choose. Out you go.'

I opened the door for her and she quietly went out. In the second session, she came back in to apologise and helped the other children learn without any distractions.

I had to let her face the natural consequence of her behaviour without recourse to any punishment. This punishment-free disciplinary action was more effective in getting the message across to her. I hope the other children who witnessed also picked up on the lesson!

Ideas for more effective forms of discipline

- Use discipline, not punishment, and the discipline must have a goal. Ask some questions, for example:

  o Why do I have to discipline my child? What do I

want to achieve by disciplining them?

  o If you want to raise a self-disciplined, responsible child, is this method of discipline effective and fit for purpose?

- One of the best forms of discipline is to let children face the natural consequences of their behaviour, once they have been duly informed and warned. The consequences must be proportionate, appropriate, and consistent with the **Three R's Rule**.[23] This states that the consequences have to be *related* to the 'misbehaviour' demonstrated, and they must be delivered in *respectful* and *reasonable* ways, without anger. For example, if a child fails to do their routine learning activity before playing their computer game, and this has already been explained to them, then instead of just saying, 'I told you the consequences, you are not allowed to play on the computer today because you didn't do your homework,' show empathy first by hugging them. Then say, 'it is really disappointing that you can't play your computer game now, until after the homework or learning activity is done.' If it's too late for them to be able to play afterwards, let them face the natural consequences but do it in love.

---

[23] From Carole and Nadim Saad (2015), *Kids Don't Come with a Manual: The Essential Guide to a Happy Family Life*, London, Best of Parenting Publishing: p 150.

o If the child is duly informed of the boundaries, the expectations, and the consequences, and the consequences are fit for purpose (that is, they follow the Three R's Rule), then be firm in implementation, showing love and no anger.

- Any disciplinary action should be motivated and stem from a place of unconditional parental love. That is, discipline should be preceded by an act of love, such as hugging the child, talking respectfully, and showing empathy and understanding.

Activities for parents

Below are some activities you can try, to internalise this strategy of effective discipline without punishment.

Physical or negative punishment may deliver immediate compliance from my child, but the long term effects are:

- ....
....

- ....
....

- ....
....

Some positive and more effective ways of discipline I can try are:

- ....
....

- ....
....

- ....
....

I will encourage my child using edifying words and statements, so that when they are in a rage they will not reach out for an object but for these encouraging words:

- Goal #1
....

- Goal #2
....

- Goal #3

....

Review: How did my child's behaviour change?

- ....

....

- ....

....

- ....

....

This takes time and effort, so be patient. Keep on trying, as this inner strength will pay off in many aspects of your life, including by building a good relationship with your child. Alternatively, you may use the goal-setting template below:

Goal-setting template

What do I want? (State the goal clearly, making it specific)	Why do I want this?	What can I do every day to move a step towards achieving the goal?	How and by when do I want to achieve this goal?

The psychological side of children in a nutshell

- Emotional intelligence is one of the single most important skills parents must master and teach their children, in order to build good relationships with them.

- Parents must help to develop the spiritual intelligence of their children, to ensure that they don't grow up to be adults with high general intelligence and emotional intelligence, but zero spiritual intelligence. However, spirituality as used here is not synonymous with religion.

- The words parents use, as well as their tone of voice, volume, attitude, and body language, can positively or negatively affect the emotions of their children. When words are used with care and love, they generate positive feelings in children and encourage them to cooperate with parents.

- Disproportionate physical punishment as a means of discipline has more long-term adverse effects on children

Notes

Chapter 5: Psychological Strategies for Parenting

In this chapter, you will be introduced to:

- How to Understand your Child

  - **Strategy No 4: Let your child feel heard and listened to**

  - Real life experience

  - Ideas for making your child feel heard and listened to

  - Activities for parents

- How to ensure cooperation, while helping your child build self confidence

  - **Strategy No 5: Empower your child by giving them the chance to choose**

  - Real life experience

  - Ideas for empowering your child by giving them a choice

  - Activities for parents

- How to build your child's confidence

  - **Strategy No 6: Use the power of praise**

  - Real life experience

- o Ideas for praising your child in the right way, so as to ensure cooperation and build their self-confidence

- o Activities for parents

- How to approach problems

  - o **Strategy No 7: Teach problem-solving skills**

  - o Real life experience

  - o How to use the problem-solving system

  - o Activities for parents

- Psychological strategies for parenting in a nutshell

How to understand your child

Strategy No 4: Let your child feel listened to

Children cannot listen to their parents until they have been listened to first. Children value your love, your time, and your undivided attention more than any of the material things you might lavish on them. Nothing can substitute for the attention and time spent listening to children.

> *A typical child may be thinking:* 'Nobody understands me, my parents don't listen. They just want to lecture me all the time with commands like, "Hey, don't do that, do this." What annoys me most is when I'm experiencing difficult feelings and they fail to acknowledge or notice it but make the frustration even worse by trying to solve the problem the way they think it needs to be solved. It makes me feel bad and that I don't want to talk to them in the future.'

Identifying with your child, acknowledging their feelings, and showing them that we understand them makes your child feel valued and significant. This also empowers them to handle negative feelings by themselves. Sometimes, all a child wants is to feel that 'someone understands me'. A parent's ability to achieve this is called empathy.

Empathy is not necessarily agreeing with the child's view, but listening, noticing, acknowledging, and tuning into the child's feelings, and resisting the temptation to probe further or start trying to solve the problem. Empathy requires listening beyond the words being spoken, and hearing instead the underlying feelings driving the actions you can see. It is about listening to both the information and the feelings, and expressing our non-judgemental acceptance.

For example, saying something simple like, 'you appear upset to have been talked to that way' can make children see that we understand and accept their feelings, that we are tuned in to them. This makes them feel connected to us. A demonstration of empathy can also be non-verbal, such as a hug.

This is how we make children feel loved, and listened to. Showing empathy this way is at the core of **emotional intelligence (EQ),** which is the very basis of effective parenting. John Gottman suggests that showing empathy in these ways, particularly when children are not on their best behaviour, does not reinforce that bad behaviour. On the contrary, accepting and respecting those feelings allows the child to self-regulate their feelings.[24] Empathy is probably the single most important thing that parents can give their children.[25]

Child psychologists unanimously agree that children's emotions must be expressed in one way or the other, and that shedding tears or bursting into laughter are both legitimate, acceptable, and harmless ways of managing, controlling and discharging difficult emotions such as anxiety, fear, anger, or sadness. These expressions of emotion do not hurt anyone or anything, but help the child process emotional distress faster. In such moments, we as parents are advised to just lend a listening ear, giving our full attention to our children. It's important that **connection** with your child always comes before **correcting** them.

---

[24] From John Gottman (1997), *Raising an Emotionally Intelligent Child,* Simon and Schuster.

[25] From Carole and Nadim Saad (2015), *Kids Don't Come with a Manual: The Essential Guide to a Happy Family Life,* London, Best of Parenting Publishing: p 121.

Teaching and correction are essential but there is a place for them. They should come in only after we have shown empathy, acknowledged the upsetting feelings, connected with our child, then, later when calmness is restored, will be the appropriate time to reaffirm the child with our unconditional love and teach and correct in love.

Real life experience

One day, one of our daughters, Andrea, complained bitterly to me.

'Dad, I don't feel you treat me fairly or the same as my sisters. They get away with saying nasty things, but I get my phone taken away if I do the same or a similar thing.' She started crying.

I simply listened to her with my full attention, saying 'Oh', 'Hmm', 'Ah', and 'I see' as she spoke to me. 'It's ok to cry,' I said. 'That must be frustrating.'

She continued sobbing.

Then I said, 'I feel sad too, and I can see how this is grossly unfair.'

She stopped crying within a few minutes.

I didn't have to give any advice or try to solve anything. I just acknowledged her feelings and my acceptance, my demonstration of understanding, and my empathy helped her to process and deal with her emotions better.

She came back after 30 minutes and said, 'Thank you for saying it's okay to cry. When you say stop crying, it makes me more upset and pushes me to cry more.'

On a separate occasion, my other, younger, daughter (Kylie) was unhappy about a sibling quarrel. Again, I acknowledged her feelings and **granted her wish in a fantasy** as follows:

'I wish I could get you sisters who would always let you have things your way. How would that feel?'

'Relaxing,' she said, already smiling.

Ideas for making your child feel heard and listened to

- Just listen. Give your child your full attention, and resist the temptation to interrupt or interject. There is no need to ask 'why?' at this stage.

- Empathise by using words like 'Oh', 'Hmm', and 'I see', or by giving a hug. Repeating back what they have told you in phrases like, 'You mean this ... happened to you?' or 'You had to suffer this...?' makes them feel that someone understands them. When children feel that their feelings have been noticed, accepted, and understood, these feelings lose their grip and begin to melt away, and the children begin to free themselves from their negative feelings.

- Resist the urge to give advice or the pressure to solve the problem for the child. Trying to solve the problem takes the opportunity to learn to solve their own problems away from the child. It also communicates a lack of confidence in them to do this on their own, which tends to be self-fulfilling in the future.

- In an empathic voice, use the 'How I wish...' phrase when their desire cannot be granted. For example, when a child comes to you crying because another child has been very nasty to them (and after the steps above have all been followed), you may say, 'How I wish I could make all children behave nicely to you.'

The above ideas help teach emotional intelligence (EQ) and help our children to learn from us. Also, EQ helps to build connection, dissipate tantrums, and divert negative feelings and their manifestations, such as worry, sadness, or whining.

Activities for parents

Below are some activities you can try to practise letting your child feel heard and listened to.

When my child talks to me, my usual initial reaction has been:

- To try as much as possible to solve the problem that is bothering them myself. Yes/no

- To ask further questions, e.g. why did you do that? Yes/no.

- Other ways:
  ....

New ways I can try to let my child feel heard and listened to are:

- ....
  ....

- ....
  ....

- ....
  ....

Review: How has my child responded to this new approach?

- ....
  ....

- ....
  ....

- ....

....

This takes time and effort, so be patient. Keep on trying, as this inner strength will pay off in many aspects of your life, including by building a good relationship with your child. Alternatively, you may use the goal-setting template below:

Goal-setting template

What do I want? (State the goal clearly, making it specific)	Why do I want this?	What can I do every day to move a step towards achieving the goal?	How and by when do I want to achieve this goal?

How to ensure cooperation, while helping your child build self confidence

Strategy No 5: Empower your child by giving them the chance to choose

You will be astonished to know that the average parent gives about 34 to 80 commands per hour[26] in their time with young children (0-12 years). This statistic is not per week, or even per day – per hour! Particularly when children are relatively young (0-8 years), most parents find themselves giving endless commands, such as:

- Wake up!

- Go to bed!

- Come for dinner!

- Wear your shoes!

- Sit down!

- Don't do ....!

- Do....!

- Stop crying!

---

[26] Carolyn Webster-Stratton (2005), *The Incredible Years*, Incredible Years: p 70.

Are you reminded of any of the above? Can you identify with any of them?

> **A typical child may be thinking:** *'Don't I deserve to have a say in my life? Can't my parents, at least, share control over my life with me? The authoritarian approach makes me want to rebel and shout "No" to their commands.'*

Developing confidence in their ability to make choices and decisions is an indispensable skill every child needs to be exposed to. In fact, there is an innate desire in every child to freely exercise their power of choice in matters that concern them. It makes them feel significant and helps build their sense of responsibility and self-esteem.

Giving children the opportunity to choose is a way to share control and it is a key strategy for avoiding many parenting problems. It helps to avoid the tendency for parents to be commanders and controllers in the home, as children do not want too many commands and orders.

There are various parenting styles, ranging from the more 'laissez-faire' or neglectful approach, through to permissive, and then to authoritative to authoritarian. As discussed in Chapter 2, a holistic or a balanced approach is known to give the best outcome. But regardless of the parenting style adopted, a dictatorship approach makes children feel pushed around, and even emotionally violated.

The natural response to orders and commands – such as 'Go to bed now' – is resistance. No one wants to be ordered about and told what to do. So instead of commanding children to go to bed, parents can offer a choice that suits them, like 'Do you want to go to bed now or in ten minutes?' This gives the power to the child to willingly embrace the offer and make the choice.

This strategy can be applied anytime parents want children to do something, whether it is at mealtime, bedtime, around household chores, shopping, getting dressing, or in a thousand other daily situations.

What if your child does not accept any of the choices that suit you? Then you must insist on choosing one of the options offered, or suggest that if they are unable to make up their mind, then you will help them choose.

Real life experience

I was busy interviewing a group of children, to select those with the musical ability and the motivation to learn to play a musical instrument in three months. In came my daughter Elizabeth, seeking attention by trying to sit on my lap, and causing a distraction in the process. I hugged her and said, 'Sweetheart, do you want to join your sister playing over there, or sit in this chair next to me? You decide,' I offered.

To my surprise and delight, she reluctantly chose to sit on the chair without questions, and she remained calm and quiet throughout the interviews with the other children.

This strategy works most of the time. When we replace commands and threats with the opportunity for the children to choose, they feel empowered and respected.

Ideas for empowering your child by giving them a choice

- Offer two or three choices that suit you (the parent). For example: 'Do you want to take your shower now or after dinner?'

- Allow the child to choose one option.

- Insist on the choices offered, or ask the child, 'If you are unable to choose, can I help you choose, or choose for you?'

Most struggles and problems are avoided when this strategy is used consistently.

Activities for parents

Below are some activities you can try to practise empowering your child by giving them the chance to choose.

When I want my child to do something, my usual way has been:

- To give a command, e.g. go and take your shower. Yes/no

- To give a warning, e.g. I want you to… Yes/no.

- Other ways:
  ....

New ways I can try to share power with my child by giving them the chance to choose:

- ....
  ....

- ....
  ....

- ....
  ....

I can implement the above ideas in the following ways:

- ....
  ....

- ....
  ....

- ....
  ....

Review after one week, and after one month. How has my child's behaviour changed?

- ....
  ....

- ....
  ....

- ....
  ....

This may require some time and effort, so be patient. Keep on trying, as this inner strength will pay off in many aspects of your life, including by building a good relationship with your child. Also, regardless of your existing skills at offering your child a choice, there is always room for improvement. Alternatively, you may use the goal-setting template below:

Goal-setting template

What do I want? (State the goal clearly, making it specific)	Why do I want this?	What can I do every day to move a step towards achieving the goal?	How and by when do I want to achieve this goal?

How to build your child's confidence

Strategy No 6: Use the power of praise

It is heart-breaking to learn the surprising fact that 80% of a typical parent's interaction with their child is made up of negative comments and criticism.[27]

> *A typical child may be thinking:* '*Instead of focusing on what I have done right and encouraging me, my parents usually find the one thing I didn't do right and make a big deal out of it. It is demoralising and demotivating to hear negative comments from my parents, the very people whose words mean a lot to me.*
> '

Another way to facilitate the development of your child's self-confidence and to encourage their cooperation is to use the power of praise. Praising, when done in the right way, has the power to encourage good behaviour. This is so because children, like every other human being, naturally yearn for appreciation, acceptance, and love. Praise tends to meet this natural craving and convert it into positive feelings, which encourage cooperation.

There are more and less effective ways of praising a child. The experts note that praise can be evaluative or descriptive. **Evaluative Praise** uses evaluative words such as telling the

---

[27] From Carole and Nadim Saad (2015), *Kids Don't Come with a Manual: The Essential Guide to a Happy Family Life*, London, Best of Parenting Publishing: p 130.

child that they are 'good', 'clever', 'excellent', 'outstanding', 'amazing', and so on. It does not emphasise the effort or the hard work expended.

The existing research proves that praising children with such words can be counterproductive and actually make the children feel afraid of failure.[28] Children may have the mindset that if they are unable to live up to the praise then they are a failure. For example, if a child is told, 'You are intelligent' when they solve a challenging mathematical problem, they may actually not want to try more challenging tasks in the future, because their inability may be perceived as 'not intelligent'. Based on recent evidence in the respected journal *Child Development*,[29] evaluative praise intended to boost children's self-esteem (also called self-inflating) can actually backfire, and be self-deflating.

The alternative, which has been found more effective, is **descriptive praise**. This focuses on describing to the child the effort, the attitude, and the hard work put into an activity, so that children can praise themselves. For example, instead of saying 'You are intelligent' when a child solves a mathematical problem, parents can describe the achievement, saying, 'You took the effort to sit down to systematically think through this? This is what I call hardworking.'

In this case, the child learns to praise themselves. More importantly, there is no evaluation, and so no associated fear of failure. The emphasis is rather on the effort and attitude, or the child's perseverance, which are fundamental for any form of

---

[28] Carol Dweck (2007), *Mindset: The New Psychology of Success*, Ballantine Books.

[29] Eddie Brummelman, Stefanie A Nelemans, Sander Thomaes, and Bram Orobio de Castro (2017), 'When Parents' Praise Inflates, Children's Self-Esteem Deflates', *Child Development*, Vol 88, No 6, pp 1799-1809.

success.

Affirming your child in their praise-worthy endeavours, and praising their effort rather than the results, will also help to build their confidence. By describing the steps involved and the effort a child has taken to achieve something, it gives them a sense of accomplishment and responsibility, and reinforces their self-belief and 'I can do it' mentality. This makes them more confident in their abilities.

For example, if your child works hard to experience a significant improvement in mathematics, parents can use descriptive praise like this one: 'This achievement in Maths is the culmination of your consistently hard work at school and at home. This shows how capable you are when you apply yourself. It makes me believe more in you. You must be proud of yourself.'

Real life experience

When she was in Year 5, my daughter Andrea worked on her vocals for her primary school X-Factor singing competition. She came so close, but did not win. She never gave up the dream but continued to work even harder the following year, when it was her last chance to compete. She managed to pull it off, and emerged as the winner. She was given a beautiful trophy and a couple of VIP tickets to the real X-Factor Live Shows at the 02 Arena in London.

My reaction was: 'This trophy and achievement represent months of your consistent hard work, practice, and ability to bounce back. It makes me think there is nothing that you cannot achieve if you apply the same consistent hard work to it. You must be proud of yourself.'

I offered this descriptive praise rather than an evaluative one, and so she learned to also praise herself.

Ideas for praising your child in the right way,

so as to ensure cooperation and build their self-confidence

- Praise their effort, their attitude, their hard work, and their perseverance, by describing what you can see they have done and how it makes you feel. For example, 'I can see you have been reading for 30 minutes with full concentration. This is what I call concentrated effort, discipline, and hard work. It makes me feel like a proud dad. You must be proud of yourself.'

- Avoid Evaluative Praise, such as 'You are good.' Rather link the 'good' achievement to the effort it took to get that result. For example, 'This award is as a result of consistent practice every day. You must be proud of yourself.'

- Avoid criticism, even when a child occasionally does not live up to your expectations. Praise their past achievements. Remember the best, and ignore the rest.

Activities for parents

Below are some activities you can try to practise the power of praise.

My usual ways of praising my child have mainly been:
- No praise at all   Yes/no

- Evaluative praise (such as 'you are clever' or 'good boy/girl') Yes/no

- Other   ways:
   ....

New ways I can try to use descriptive praise are:
- ....
  ....

- ....
  ....

- ....
  ....

I can implement the above ideas when my child has done/achieved things like:
- ....
  ....

- ....
  ....

- ....
  ....

Review after one week, and after one month. How has my

child's behaviour changed in response to this new approach?

- ....
....

- ....
....

- ....
....

Changing behaviour takes time and effort, so remember to be patient. Keep on trying, as this inner strength will pay off in many aspects of your life, including by building a good relationship with your child. Also, regardless of your skill at using descriptive praise, there is always room for improvement. Alternatively, you might prefer to use the goal-setting template below:

Goal-setting template

What do I want? (State the goal clearly, making it specific)	Why do I want this?	What can I do every day to move a step towards achieving the goal?	How and by when do I want to achieve this goal?

How to approach problems

Strategy No 7: Teaching problem-solving skills

One of the best skills parents can pass on to their children is the ability to solve problems.

It is natural for parents to want to solve problems for their children. The difficulty with this is that, apart from robbing the children of the opportunity to learn from their own mistakes and develop their confidence, we also communicate the implication that they are incapable and incompetent. And this tends to become self-fulfilling.

> ***A typical child may be thinking:*** *'It usually seems like my parents have lost confidence in me when they want to do everything for me without consulting me at all in things that are important to me. What discourages me most is when they try to fix my problems for me. It makes me feel I'm incompetent and cannot be expected to do anything well.'*

It is important that parents do not help their children become helpless. One example of this is you doing your child's school work for them.

Problem-solving is also a strategy for conflict resolution in general, as it helps to resolve conflicts amicably and encourage cooperation from children. The unique feature of this strategy is that it appears to combine many of the preceding strategies – it acknowledges feelings, helps both parties feel heard, and allows children to exercise their power to choose by participating in the process of brainstorming ideas and making the final decision.

Real life experience

When we first bought a smartphone for one of our daughters, Andrea, she starting being too influenced by peers and friends around the world on social media. We gave her some gentle hints about both the benefits and dangers of social media and becoming hooked on her phone all the time, but after her 10th birthday we trusted her to manage her usage by herself.

The adverse effects became apparent very quickly. Her language, attitude and behaviour towards us (her parents) changed for the worse. So we warned her that if this negative attitude continued, she was going to lose her right to use her phone.

The warning made no difference, so we ended up confiscating the phone for a day. The next day, she politely asked, 'Please can I have my phone?'

'Sure,' I said. 'If you can come up with a plan or a way that will work for all of us, so that you have your phone and we all have dignity and respect for each other in this family.'

Surprisingly, she quickly drafted a contract with penalties for non-compliance:

First offence, seize the phone for a day. For the second time, take the phone away for a week, and on the third offence, keep the phone until further notice.

'Can we add not insisting on going out with friends we don't know, except if absolutely necessary?' I asked, which she happily added to the list of things she was going to do differently.

We both signed and pasted it somewhere on the noticeboard in the kitchen. The problem has never reoccurred.

When we get children involved in generating solutions to problems they are part of, they take responsibility and ownership of it and it works very well most of the time.

How to use the problem-solving system

1. Clearly identify and define the problem or the conflict that needs to be solved by:

    a. First listening and noticing the child's feelings. For example, 'I can see you are unhappy about...' (Please refer to **Strategy No. 4: Let your child feel heard and listened to**).

    b. State your feelings about it. For example, 'The problem is that this issue (name it) makes me feel...'

    c. So, there is a problem, how do we solve it?

2. Work together with the child (3+ years) to generate a list of ideas as an alternative solution.

    a. No idea is ruled out at this stage of brainstorming.

    b. The child should be encouraged to lead this process with the parent making their own suggestions.

    c. All ideas should preferably be written down or noted.

3. Evaluate the list of ideas, choosing which ones are practical and have less negative implications.

    a. Parents can ask: 'What do you think about that?', 'How will that work?' etc.

    b. Rule out ideas that you are not comfortable with, using a justification or reason.

4. Decide on the best, mutually-acceptable idea (solution), and work out ways to implement it.

5. Put the solution into specific plans of action that answers the 'what, who, how, when, what if' questions. For example:

   a. What needs to be done?

   b. Who is responsible for what?

   c. How should it be done?

   d. By when should it be done?

   e. What if one forgets their part or is unable to pull their weight, how should they be reminded of their responsibility, and what are the ways to get them back on track?

6. Review and reward (please refer to the section in Strategy No 6 on descriptive praise), or provide support if needed.

Activities for parents

Below are some activities you can try to practise the problem-solving approach.

My usual response to conflicts or problems has been to:

- Try as much as possible to solve the problem for my child. Yes/no

- Quickly suggest a solution.   Yes/no

- Let my child take care of it.   Yes/no

- Sweep the issue under the carpet or leave it.   Yes/no

- Other   ways:
  ....

Situations where I can try to use problem-solving skills are:

- ....
  ....

- ....
  ....

- ....
  ....

How to implement the above ideas in the face of a conflict or problem:

- ....
  ....

- ....

  ....

- ....

  ....

Review after one week, and again after one month. How has my child's behaviour changed in response to this new approach?

- ....

  ....

- ....

  ....

- ....

  ....

Changing behaviour takes time and effort, so remember to be patient. Keep on trying, as this inner strength will pay off in many aspects of your life, including by building a good relationship with your child. Also, regardless of your skill at using the problem-solving system, there is always room for improvement. Alternatively, you might prefer to use the goal-setting template below:

Goal-setting template

What do I want? (State the goal clearly, making it specific)	Why do I want this?	What can I do every day to move a step towards achieving the goal?	How and by when do I want to achieve this goal?

Psychological strategies for children in a nutshell

- Children are unable to listen to parents until they feel heard and understood first.

- Empathy as an expression of emotional intelligence (EQ) is the way to make children feel that they have been listened to and understood.

- The key to empathising with a child is to accept and validate their feelings.

- Many parental problems can be resolved when parents share power by giving their children the chance to choose rather than issuing commands.

- Descriptive praise is the best way to affirm a child and encourage good behaviour and habits.

- One of the best ways to ensure cooperation from children and help them build their self-confidence is to teach them problem-solving skills. Parents should involve children in finding solutions to the problems they cause, so that they see themselves as part of any solution.

Notes

Chapter 6: The Essential Values for Children

In this chapter, you will be introduced to:

- The importance of values

- What are values? What is a core value system?

- Real life experience

- A list of some essential values

- Working with the more important values

  - Love

  - Purpose

  - Responsibility

  - Critical and Creative Thinking

  - Discipline

  - Resilience/confidence

  - Excellence

  - Appreciation

  - Attitude

- The Essential Values for Children in a nutshell

The importance of values

The ideas in this section are adapted principally from the teachings of one of my mentors, Dr Sunday Adelaja (DSA). I have used his online resources on parenting,[30] which he has granted me his full and generous permission to use, as the basis of this chapter.

When it comes to raising children, our primary concern should be what we leave *for* them, but what we leave *inside* them. As important as material things are, it is far more important to instil a core value system in our children. With the right core value system or mindset, they will have what it takes to create, maintain, and enjoy the material assets we may bequeath to them.

Values encourage good habits in children, and these good and productive habits will propel them forward to greatness in life. Without a strong value system or a strong spine (to use the human body as a metaphor), children are unable to even maintain any wealth we might leave for them. Without a strong value system, misuse and abuse can become almost inevitable. Just observe children hooked on drugs – most of them have access to great material wealth, but they are being controlled by it, rather than knowing how to control it themselves.

What are values? What is a core value system?

---

[30] I would like to thank Dr Sunday Adelaja (DSA) for this permission. His audio series on parenting, along with other useful teaching sets on topics such as financial success, relationships, analytical (critical) thinking, purpose, and many more, are freely available on www.youtube.com/sundayadelajaofficial.

The UK as a nation shares certain fundamental values around respect and freedom of expression, including:

- democracy,

- the rule of law,

- individual liberty,

- mutual respect,

- tolerance of those with different faiths and beliefs and for those without faith.

From the perspective of parenting, core values can in my view be defined as our guiding principles or what we value in life. They encompass what we classify as good and desirable, and help form our beliefs, reflect our attitudes, and dictate our behaviour.

In Chapter 2, I discussed an important concept parents may not be aware of: the fundamental purpose of parenting. DSA passionately reiterates that the purpose of parenting is to *guide the child to develop character and a set of core values inside of them in order to become a unique personality.* 'Personality' here means the true person they were created to be, so that they can stand on their own two feet in life and serve humanity with their gifts, leaving this world in a better condition than they found it.

The core value system and worldview of a child is the anchor that holds them in place. It serves as a beacon, a navigation system, and a compass, so that when the wind of difficulty blows, they can always return to facing in the right direction. Children will certainly make mistakes, but those with strong value systems instilled in them always find their way back, just like the compass.

A child without a value system is likely to grow up to become just a biological mass, driven only by emotions, instincts, and reflexes. According to DSA, this is the 'animalistic' level of living, or living as our 'lower self'.

Such children tend to have only a materialistic worldview – if they cannot see or feel something in the moment, it is not a reality. There is no recognition of eternal and invisible values, such as ideas or thoughts, integrity, kindness, and spirituality, which are what give birth to our material possessions.

Am I saying that feelings are bad? No. This would contradict the ideas and lessons in Chapter 4: **The Psychological side of children**, and Chapter 5: **Psychological strategies for parenting**. This section on values is not denying the need for feelings, but it is challenging the notion that feelings and emotions are all there is to a human being.

There is a spiritual side (please refer to **Psychology vs Spirituality** in Chapter 4) to every human being, and this is where our personal power lies. Those who are spiritually intelligent can use this power to harness their emotions. They are able to choose their thoughts, which in turn determine their feelings. The idea is to pay attention to feelings, but not to allow negative feelings to dominate your life.

Feelings come and go, after all. Acknowledging, accepting, and respecting children's feelings is a good start if you want to secure their cooperation and to avoid having them become discouraged, with all the associated emotional wounds. And once children feel understood, the next step is to work on forming their values, as a guiding light to live by. When challenges find our children – and they will – it is these values inside them that will help them not to bow to peer pressure or be swayed from their convictions. Instead, they will be able to withstand pressure, confront life, and emerge triumphant.

The development of a value system starts with a child's parents. It is up to us as parents to develop a strong world view and value system first, so that we are able to pass this on to our children. Sending children to school and religious classes may be necessary and helpful, but the lessons learned from such institutions may still prove insufficient for preventing children from becoming a mere 'biomass'. Parents need a programme, a routine, and a system to intentionally address and shape the personality inside their children.

Forming your child's value system cannot be left up to chance. The teaching of value systems needs to be a structured process, to be carried out intentionally and consistently.

An appropriate and proportionate structure is excellent for enhancing children's productivity, as a result of the good habits associated with it. These include discipline, concentration, and hard work.

However, occupying children with too many structured activities can stifle their freedom to exercise their imagination, creativity, and ingenuity. These are all qualities that usually stem from free time, when the child is allowed to explore what they really love to do. So the right balance between structure and freedom needs to be found and struck.

Real life experience

My own experience of trying to instil some values into our children has led me to compile a list of ideas. This list is written pasted up on a board, where everyone can easily read it when we hold our regular weekly family meetings. This is what our list says:

1. Formal education may give me a certificate and a living, but self-education will give me success and a fortune plus happiness.
2. Everyone has a life purpose in this world, and my job is to discover and develop mine through self-education. This is where my true fulfilment is hidden and is waiting for me.
3. I will write my dream/goal down with a deadline or timescale, making it SMART (Specific, Measurable, Achievable, Relevant and Time-bound).

4. A dream or goal written down clearly, along with timed action plans, is a goal 75% accomplished.
5. Acting on my dreams daily, using hard work and without procrastination or excuses, makes my dreams come true.
6. Everyone is born with unimaginable wealth buried inside them. The tools to convert this into riches are self, purpose, time, space, and work.
7. I need to spend about 10,000 hours (3 hours a day, for 10 years) in self-development, if I am to become my very best at my life purpose. Therefore, time is the most important resource I have. I can choose to waste it, or I can invest it towards this 10,000-hour threshold to become an expert in anything I set my heart on.
8. There are no failures in life. People who see or think of failure are only those who don't know the secrets above, or do know them but are not willing to pay the price to become successful.

At every meeting, we try to relate the topic being discussed to one of the above ideas. Sometimes, we concentrate on just one idea for several weeks.

A list of some essential values

Some of the most important values that must be instilled in children are:

- Love/consideration/empathy/kindness/respect
- Purpose
- Responsibility
- Discipline/diligence/hard work/patience
- Excellence
- Resilience/determination/perseverance/confidence

- Passion/zeal

- Critical and creative thinking

- Appreciation/gratitude/honouring one's own parents and the parents of others

- Attitude towards money/time/authority/governments/law and order.

- Integrity/honesty

- Justice/fairness/equity

- Generosity/giving

Working with the more important values

In this chapter, I will take you through some of the most important values, along with simple ways to instil these values in your child.

Love

The human spirit originates with the Creator, who is the source of all love. It must be communicated to children continuously and from an early stage that God loves them, regardless of their actions or imperfections. Bad deeds prevent us from receiving this unconditional love, which is extended from the Creator to all of humanity.

The most important thing is to help your child to embrace this unconditional love, reciprocate by loving God in return, and translate this love into loving other fellow human beings, irrespective of their differences and shortcomings. Love is the greatest value, because a genuine love for people will be demonstrated in acts of kindness, empathy, compassion, respect, and in almost all of the other values.

Children must be exposed to the idea that love, in the sense of God's unconditional love and acceptance, is the greatest value possible. It is in our human nature to love others and to receive love in return. Hatred is unnatural to any human being, and generates only bad feelings.

One of the greatest gifts parents can give to their children is to raise them to be content with themselves, to have high self-esteem, and to value themselves. When children value themselves, they also value other people, and treat them in the same way they want to be treated. This accomplishment is a far better legacy for your children than any material possessions.

Firstly, children should be helped to accept that they are loved by the Creator of the universe and all other human beings, and this only works if they accept and love themselves no matter their imperfections.

Second, children should be helped to understand that every human being, regardless of age, country of birth, disabilities, beliefs, or preferences, are of equal value and deserve to be accepted and loved, and treated with honour, dignity, and respect. Children should also expect to be treated as equals.

This does not mean equal in terms of age, experience, possessions, and so on, but with regards to dignity and respect, and how they deserve unconditional love and a sense of significance.

Thirdly, children should be taught that no-one is an island. We are all connected, such that what one person cannot do or have can be found in another, usually someone close to them, and the key to accessing this is love. We all need one another.

When a child grows up without a sense of love as a value

A child without the core value of love instilled in them grows up with a feeling of insecurity. They find it difficult to accept themselves. As a result, they hate themselves, and they are often mad at their parents, mad at teachers, mad at governments and systems, mad at the world and life in general, and so have no respect for life or property.

Our prisons are full of people without the value of love for self and others. When this happens, it is costly to the individual, the family, and society. There is a cost even to keeping them in prison in these extreme cases. The damage done to others and their family can be incalculable. So parenting without recourse to value systems has both huge personal and societal costs.

You may check the homicide rate in your town, city or country and look into the root causes for yourself. The UK's Office for National Statistics reports that there were 571 homicides – that is, people murdered or killed by other people – from March 2015 to March 2016.[31] This includes teenagers killing other

---

[31] From The Office for National Statistics - online: https://www.ons.gov.uk/peoplepopulationandcommunity/crimeandjustice/com

teenagers, particularly in London. It could be inferred that most of the perpetrators were raised without this core value of love. As a result, they are driven by emotions of anger and hatred.

How to help your child love and accept themselves, and extend this love to other people

- Treat your child as an equal in terms of dignity. Parents should never treat their children as less than themselves. We are all offspring of the Creator, and share His image and spirit, irrespective of our size or age. When parents treat children with respect, children will respond by respecting themselves, their parents, and other people.

- Please refer to Chapter 2: **The Essential need for Love**, and offer undivided attention, affection, and affirmation to your child.

- Offer descriptive praise to your child (refer to **Strategy No 6: Using the Power of Praise** for more).

- Help your child to translate the act of loving God into loving people. This must be done, because every human being shares the nature of God.

pendium/focusonviolentcrimeandsexualoffences/yearendingmarch2016/homicide

Purpose

Another essential value is a sense of purpose, and the notion that no life is an accident. Children should be taught that there is a reason for their life here on earth, and that during any particular season in their lives there is at least one main assignment that will reflect the highest expression of themselves. The Creator does not release a life to this earth without a purpose, no matter the circumstances surrounding their birth.

A child with a sense of purpose is able to live for something greater than themselves and rise above their 'lower self'. They are better able to avoid the tendency to be controlled only by emotions and feelings, and instead try to exercise their will and inner power to express their potential, creativity, and uniqueness.

Your child needs to know that there are different views about life. The atheists' view supported by evolutionary evidence sees life as having no sense of purpose. Creationist scientists, backed by facts in nature and 'experiential' evidence that cannot be subject to scientific tests in the laboratory, accept that there must be a Creator to make the complexities and the orderliness with which the universe functions, and even why humans can conduct scientific enquiries to make sense of the world. Creationist scientists embrace the biblical account of creation and are of the view that the human life, just like any 'scientific matter', cannot die but instead goes on to exist in a different form.

This is consistent with the idea that every human being is released from the spiritual realm into this physical realm by the Creator, as an answer to a particular problem facing humanity in a particular sphere of life. It also means that when we leave this realm, it is not the end – we simply return to the spiritual realm where we came from, to give an account of our time on Earth.

Our purpose is usually hidden in our gifts, talents, abilities, uniqueness, the way we are shaped, and so forth.

Our greatest source of motivation for living is to lead a life with purpose. A purpose is something we are good at, and which makes life better for other people. In other words, it solves a problem or provides an answer to an issue in life.

Purpose gives meaning to life. It provides us with fuel, and the energy to live with a smile even in the midst of challenges and difficulties. This is why it is so important to help your child discover their purpose, and tailor their education to develop their skills so that they might effectively fulfil this purpose to the best of their abilities.

When a child grows up without a sense of purpose as a value

Without a sense of purpose, a child is unable to live their highest (best) self or discover who they truly are – which is, after all, where their purpose lies hidden. This means they grow up living from pay-cheque to pay-cheque, without planning, existing only within a survivalist mindset.

Also, in the absence of purpose, the child's only focus is on themselves. They worry about what other people think or say about them more than anything else, asking, 'What do I look like? What are they thinking about me? What's in it for me?'

In the worst cases, this can potentially drive some children to suicide. It also means that their primary concern is 'personal safety', rather than standing up for their convictions and against evil or wrongdoings in society. This idea is highlighted in a famous quote by Martin Luther King, Jr: 'If a man has not discovered something that he will die for, he isn't fit to live.'[32]

---

[32] From https://www.brainyquote.com/quotes/martin_luther_king_jr_101378

How to help your child discover their purpose in life

- Observe your child over time and pick up the clues from their natural responses to life – responses which if developed will be good for him/her, good for other people, will serve the greater good, and make this world a better place. Why is this a good approach? Your child's purpose is buried inside them, so do not look anywhere else for the answers. You child will naturally tend to gravitate towards their purpose if too many distractions are not placed in their way.

- Expose your child to many activities and observe their natural inclinations. Ask yourself the following questions:

    o What is he/she naturally good at, without any formal training?

    o What does he/she naturally gravitate towards?

    o What does he/she have a deep passion for?

    o What does he/she enjoy most?

- The above approach is particularly applicable to very young children (3-7 years). For relatively older children (from 8-18 years), allow them time alone to listen to their 'inner GPS', as their purpose is wrapped up in their gifts and is therefore buried inside them. Asking them for an honest answer to the following question may give you a huge clue as to their purpose:

    o If all occupations paid the same salary, and this was enough that money was not an issue, what would you want to do with your time and life?

- What if a child is immensely gifted in two areas, for example in sports and in music? My advice is to let them develop at both. With time, they will naturally gravitate towards the one that will be the highest expression of themselves.

- What if your child does not seem to find their rhythm in anything? Don't be concerned – there is certainly something they are good at. They just need to be encouraged to look for it within. I am hugely impressed by how Nick Vujicic, born with no limbs, was able to discover his purpose to become the world's most extraordinarily sensational speaker. You can also encourage your child to become busy, occupying themselves with productive pursuits. This will give them the opportunity to discover their skills and interests.

Activities to try to help discover a child's purpose

My child is naturally good at:

- ....
....
- ....
....

My child naturally gravitates towards:

- ....
....
- ....
....

My child shows the following talents (gifts) in their playing activities:

- ....
....
- ....
....
- ....
....

The talents (gifts or traits) shown can be developed and used to solve the following problems or make life better for society in the following ways:

- ....
....

- ....
....

- ....
....

I can help my child develop their talents (gifts or traits) in the following ways:

- ....
....

- ....
....

- ....
....

Responsibility

Another important value children should be introduced to is a sense of responsibility – that is, their ability to respond to events that happen to them with the awareness that their response can determine the ultimate outcome.

Babies are helpless and are totally dependent on their parents, at least in their first year after birth. This complete dependency can make children grow up to be reliant and feel entitled to a 'good life' without any making effort of their own. Gradually weaning them from this entitlement mindset at the appropriate age is vitally important.

Children should also be made aware that their family's goal in supporting them is to equip them to be able to take 100% responsibility for their choices, actions, and life. They also need to learn how their choices or actions affect themselves and others.

For example, good choices such as cultivating the discipline to study hard have tremendous benefits for their own life and those of others. Conversely, negative choices such as getting into bad company or doing drugs will have negative consequences, and those consequences can potentially wreck or ruin their own lives and the lives of others.

As soon as children are able to appreciate things, they should be taught the real truth: that they are the only person who can determine the quality of their life, and the level of their happiness and joy. They do this through their actions, and complaining or blaming other people, including their parents, is a complete waste of time because it puts the responsibility on another person, someone they have no control over. They need to realise that the freedom to have absolute control over their thoughts and actions is enough to help them determine their desired outcomes.

One of the most important lessons I learned during my difficulties (Chapter 1) was my discovery that nothing would change until I took 100% responsibility through my thoughts and actions.

This idea is profoundly illustrated in Jack Canfield's model[1] for success in general, which we covered in Chapter 1:

E + R = O
Events + Response = Outcome

This formula simply shows that any result or **outcome (O)** in our lives is determined by two forces:

1. **The events (E):** which we have almost no control over, and which happens to us and others equally – for example, the weather, economic hardships, or accidents.

2. **Our response (R):** which we have absolute control over, through our thoughts and actions (or inaction) following these events.

Is it the events or our response that has more impact on our lives? In the words of Dr Dennis Kimbro, 'Life is 10% what happens to us and 90% how we react to it.'[33]

Thankfully, we have absolute control over our responses, and we can teach our children that they can also learn to choose their response to even the most difficult and challenging events in life. In this way, they can influence their outcomes and their quality of life.

---

[33] From http://www.famous-quotes-and-quotations.com/dennis_p_kimbro.html.

By focusing on and using a positive response, the outcome becomes known in advance. Life is no longer a mystery but very much predictable. This is how we help our children take control over their lives, rather than allowing life to control them.

Parents should allow their children to start to learn taking responsibility by offering them choices, instead of merely issuing commands and orders, which also makes children feel pushed about. Please refer back to **Strategy No 5: Empowering your child by giving the chance to choose,** and **Strategy No 7: Teaching Problem-Solving Skills** in Chapter 5 for more on this.

When a child grows up without a sense of responsibility as a value system

Without this value, a child grows up with an entitlement mindset. They blame their parents, others, or society for their lack of anything in life. When these feelings are allowed to fester, they turn to anger and become damaging to the self, others, and society as a whole.

Children with no sense of responsibility also have no sense of boundaries and no control over their difficult emotions, including anger.

How to help your child develop a sense of responsibility

- No blaming: teach your child never to blame anyone for, not even themselves, for what happens, but to learn from the experience and positively respond to the events. Asking the following questions may help:

    o What can you do to influence the outcome of this event?

    o After reacting to an event, ask, 'What did you do

right? And how can you make it better next time around?'

- o Never ask, 'What did you do wrong?' This makes us focus on the negative, giving power and strength to what is being focused on.

- Encourage autonomy: trust your child with age-appropriate responsibilities. If things don't go right at first, encourage them and provide support.

  - o Entrusting children with responsibilities should be done incrementally, from small responsibilities right up to more major ones. For example, our eldest daughter was initially trusted to buy her own school supplies, and later trusted to order supplies for the whole family. This progression helped build her competence and confidence at this skill, and to take on increasing levels of responsibility.

  - o Allow the child to make mistakes (if deemed not dangerous or fatal), and to learn from the experience. Apart from exposing them to the consequences of their actions, this autonomy teaches them to be self-reliant and builds confidence in their own abilities.

Activities to try to internalise responsibility as a value in your child

List some things that you have been doing for your child that they are capable of doing themselves. (For example, feeding themselves, making their bed, doing their homework, or taking charge of their shopping, depending on the age of the child.)

- ....
  ....

- ....
  ....

- ....
  ....

Plan to let your child try these (age-appropriate) ideas listed above, to help develop their competence, confidence and self-reliance.

Record your child's responses:

- ....
  ....

- ....
  ....

- ....
  ....

Review: was it too much or overwhelming for your child?

- ....
  ....

- ....
  ....

- ....
  ....

How can you make it better?

- ....
  ....

- ....
  ....

- ....
  ....

Critical and Creative Thinking

Another indispensable value a child must be helped to absorb is a developed mind. That is, the ability to nurture creative thinking, critical thinking, analytical thinking, productive ways to process information, as well as the ability to evaluate issues in life.

Every child, and for that matter, every human being, thinks. It is natural to think. However, critical or creative thinking does not come naturally to humans. This skill has to be intentionally developed, otherwise our default thinking can be shallow, distorted, biased, or prejudiced, limiting children's ability to objectively and fairly process information to aid their progress in life.

Critical thinking is not synonymous with criticising, although the two are not mutually exclusive either. Critical thinking goes far beyond just critiquing and looking at the potential drawbacks.

Critical thinking is the ability to look at an issue from different angles so as to establish a balanced view. It allows us to weigh up issues and look at arguments from both sides – examining and evaluating their relative strengths and weaknesses, the evidence that supports these positions, the underlying assumptions, and the implications and conclusions drawn – and come up with creative recommendations for improvement.

Children need to learn how to think creatively and critically if they are to solve problems logically. Below are some ideas about critical thinking:

- *Critical thinking requires mental effort.* It is careful and intentional thinking, giving thoughtful and reasoned consideration to a claim, in order to assess if it is true or not.

- *Critical thinking is logical.* It follows a rational thought process to arrive at a conclusion or a judgement about a particular idea (not a person). It helps us to question whether we agree or disagree with a claim we have heard, read, or seen, instead of just accepting an unsubstantiated claim ('inherited opinion').

- *Critical thinking encourages children to ask questions.* Such questions include: What? How? Why? What if? how did you know that? It encourages us not to accept claims at face value, 'inherit' opinions, or accept ideas or information just because someone told us to.

- *Critical thinking encourages professional scepticism* as a useful exercise, to question everything and analyse all the available evidence.

- *Critical thinking also comes from the premise that human beings are not perfect.* As a result, every issue that involves people will have two sides, which should both be appraised critically.

- *Critical thinking adds value*, by making a contribution or offering alternatives as an improvement on what has been criticised.

- *Critical thinking does not rule out making decisions based on emotion, intuition, or faith,* but it examines the reasonability of doing so.

- *Critical thinking helps to sort relevant information* from irrelevant information, and to make better decisions. If developed, it should therefore help children to cope with life better.

Critical thinking simply follows the Scientific Method, which includes the following steps:

1. A question is asked or a problem is identified.

2. A hypothesis is formulated based on observation.

3. Relevant data is collected.

4. The hypothesis is tested logically against the data.

5. Logical and reliable conclusions are drawn.

Using the scientific method makes critical thinkers ask questions, gather relevant data, and logically subject the question to examination against the evidence, in order to arrive at logical conclusions to help understand the matter in question and the universe as a whole. This way children will have and live by '**informed opinions**' rather than unquestionably accept others' opinions as the truth ('**inherited opinions**').

Critical thinking should, therefore, be a life-long pursuit for children. This is because none of us are born with the natural ability to think critically.

See **Strategy No 7: Teaching Problem-Solving Skills**, in Chapter 5, as one way to help your child to use their mind strategically and creatively, by generating relevant solutions to problems. Problem-solving also affords children the opportunity to use their imagination, a powerful aspect of the mind. The school system may not help develop this part of the mind, which is the source of all innovation and inventions, because it may tell children *what* to think rather than *how* to think. All innovations and inventions began in the minds of people, from Henry Ford through to Steve Jobs, Bill Gates, and Mark Zuckerberg.

When a child grows up without a sense of critical and creative thinking as a value system

Without the ability to develop their mental faculties and think critically, children are reduced to living by their feelings and instincts alone. This is the animalistic level of living, which limits their progress. This lower level or 'survivalist thinking' is characterised by prejudice, biasness, distortion, and shallow-mindedness. Children stuck at this level will fall prey to deception, delusion, and superstition. They will follow the crowd instead of their own convictions.

For example, they may take actions without an informed reason for them, such as getting married, giving birth to children, or following their peers and friends. Such children tend to be driven by the opinions of peers, taking the viewpoints of others' (inherited opinion) as their own, without any effort on their part to check for an independent and justified viewpoint. Thinking requires mental effort, and many children would rather die than think critically and creatively!

The lack of this value produces shallow children, who follow the mass media without questioning anything. Once they hear news and rumours, they assume and imply truth, and therefore have no need for verification of the facts.

How to help your child develop critical and creative thinking skills

- Teach your child *how* to think rather than *what* to think.

- Ask questions to identify your child's thought processes.

- Encourage your child to look at both sides of every issue. Why? Because each side may have strengths and weaknesses, and no side is 100% perfect.

- Encourage your child to question everything, or seek evidence or answers for themselves. The quality of their questions determines the quality of the answers they will get. Parents should not see the questioning of ideas by children as a rebellion or a defiance of their authority. You should actually commend your children for daring to exert the mental effort to use their mind in a creative way.

In this way, critical thinking becomes the norm for them.

- When children ask questions, parents should allow them the opportunity to explore the answer for themselves first. For example, a good response to a child's question can be, 'That is an interesting question. What do you think?'

Let me briefly illustrate how some degree of critical thinking can be applied to a statement like 'Africans are poor.' The majority of people, who do not apply critical thinking, will accept this statement as true without questioning it. However, someone with a developed mind will ask a number of questions:

- Who are 'Africans' in this context? Is it just people living in the continent of Africa, or do they include people living anywhere in the world who are of African descent?

- What does 'poor' mean? Is it material wealth? Is it referring to absolute poverty or relative poverty?

Just asking a few questions like this will help switch your critical thinking on, to better process the information. Some of the outcomes of this thinking may include:

- Not all Africans are poor.

- There is relative poverty in every country, even the richest countries on earth.

- Africans living on the African continent may also be 'rich' in other ways. For example, they may be happier, more resilient, and so on. (You may check the suicide rate in the developed world versus that of the developing world for yourself. According to a Euronews report on the 18th of May 2017, Europe is the region with the highest rate of suicide in the world, while the Eastern Mediterranean region has the lowest.[34])

The logical conclusion is that the statement is not totally true, and one can choose to disagree, having looked at both sides and the supporting evidence.

---

[34] From Euronews website, 'Suicide rate is highest in Europe: UN health agency report,' http://www.euronews.com/2017/05/18/suicide-rate-is-highest-in-europe-un-health-agency-report.

Activities to try to internalise critical and creative thinking skills as a value in your child

As part of normal day-to-day conversations with the child, ask questions, such as:

- Why do you want to wear these clothes/shoes at this time (summer, winter) of the year?

- Why do you prefer eating _____ for breakfast?

Then try to listen to what your child says, because the answer is not as important as the thought processes and the logic used to arrive at their decision. Is their reasoning supported by evidence?

- Ask your child if they can spot any problem, drawback or limitations with their chosen side or decision. This will help them look at the other side of an argument.

- Make a list of questions you want to ask your child today/this week:

- ....
  ....

- ....
  ....

- ....
  ....

Review: What was your child's response? Does your child have a strong 'why', backed by their own found evidence?

- ....
....

- ....
....

- ....
....

How can you make this experience more effective and help your child with critical thinking skills?

- ....
....

- ....
....

- ....
....

Discipline

There can be no sustainable success in life without discipline, hard (and smart) work, diligence, and the exercise of patience. There is no shortcut or a substitute for these fundamental values.

Discipline in this context is the capacity to carry out one's intentions without excuses or procrastination. Simply put, discipline is doing those things you plan and say you want to do, and which are good for you, good for others, and serve the greater good. It means doing these things even if you don't feel like doing them. Discipline relies greatly on inner strength and willpower.

Olympic champions, famous footballers, and top musicians – to mention just a few – all must discipline themselves to become skilful at their craft. Without this discipline, there can be no success.

Children should have these values ingrained in them if they are to stand a better chance of making the most of their lives. Today, many things – TV, social media, phones, the internet, and so on – are screaming for our attention. It is incredibly difficult for anyone, especially the younger generation, to discipline themselves to sit down, shut off all distractions, and concentrate on one productive activity for an hour.

If as parents we can encourage our children to do this, then they will be set up for success in life. It will be relatively easy for them to say no to good things, so that they can say yes to great things.

It is a good idea for parents to have a structured schedule for children to follow, so that they can learn the practise of discipline, hard work, and diligence. The greatest discipline is dedicating time to master one's thoughts and fully concentrate on one thing, in order to practise or to improve at something. When children learn to focus on one thing consistently over a long time, the genius inside them is released.

Discipline involves pain, inconvenience, and discomfort. It means pushing yourself through beneficial routines, preferably at fixed times every day, for optimal results in learning, exercising, rehearsing, and so on. If followed properly, this fixed routine helps instil an indispensable habit for success: sitting down to concentrate.

But people generally do not like pain. In fact, children will do anything to avoid the pain associated with discipline. Children need to be helped to understand and accept that success in life comes from some of the very actions that require pain.

This idea is captured in the statement of Mohammed Ali, one of the greatest boxing personalities of all time: 'I don't count my sit-ups. I only start counting when it starts hurting. When I feel pain, that's when I start counting, because that's when it really counts.' This reflects the popular saying, 'no pain, no gain.'

Just remember that the pain that comes from a lack of discipline in life is far greater than the voluntary pain associated with discipline. The pain we experience from a lack of discipline is an involuntary, self-inflicted pain, manifesting in failure, mediocrity, poverty, ignorance, and imprisonment. For every 2 grams of pain we suffer from discipline, we can avoid 2 tons of pain from indiscipline. Discipline demands continuous, never-ending self-education and improvement. It takes discipline to pursue one's purpose, or any goal in life.

When a child grows up without a sense of discipline as a value system

Most productive things children can do, such as learning something or practising a skill, are uncomfortable and painful. It takes discipline to consistently do such useful things. When discipline is not formed in a child, they will try to avoid pain at all cost. Their mindset becomes: 'Do it if it feels good, avoid it otherwise.'

Trapped in this way of thinking, children are unable to sit

down and concentrate on something productive for a reasonable length of time. They easily become distracted by outside influences, such as social media, phones, friends, TV, or the internet.

And without discipline, children will continue to opt for instant gratification. They cannot delay it and see far into the future. They want things now, and therefore miss out on all the good things that only come over time and with long-term effort.

Real life experience

Recently, when the children were on a short break from school, I provided an incentive for Andrea to start reading personal development books. I showed her a range of books and offered to give her £10 for each book she is able to prove to me that she has finished reading. To my surprise, she finished reading "*Money Won't Make You Rich*" in just a couple of days. I asked her a few questions to verify her reading and to see evidence of a list of 5 lessons learned, and handed in her cash reward. Her younger siblings are also encouraged and challenged to follow suit.

Why am I doing this?

- It will instil discipline - a habit for success in life

- It gives them a sense of achievement

- It teaches them that money is earned by work

- It gives them the opportunity to learn how to manage money

The incentive doesn't necessarily have to be money. It could be extra playing time with friends, or an activity the children enjoy most. If it's money, then the right amount to really incentivise the children to want to go the extra mile depends on your own personal circumstances with your children. Also, the means of instilling discipline doesn't necessarily have to be about reading books. It could be any useful and beneficial craft or activity that requires discipline to focus.

How to help your child develop discipline, hard work and diligence

- Create a daily routine. This might be a one-hour homework or self-education time, at a fixed time each day, such as from 7pm to 8pm. Remember the 10,000-hour rule – anything a person spends 10,000 hours doing, improving on, learning, practising, exploring, or researching, they will master.

- Initially, you may meet some resistance, so you could try starting with 15 minutes, increasing this gradually to 30 minutes, until your child has the stamina needed for a full hour.

- For younger children, you can read to them or engage them in any age-appropriate activities. For more independent children, you can set them to do their homework, read, or any self-learning activity by themselves. The aim is to develop their ability to concentrate on one thing for an hour.

- What if children don't want to cooperate? Please refer to **Strategy No 5: Empower your child by giving the chance to choose**, and **Strategy No 7: Teach problem-solving skills**, both found in Chapter 5.

Activities to try to internalise discipline, hard work, and diligence in your child

List some activities you can help your child to do, to help them to develop discipline:

- ....
....

- ....
....

- ....
....

Plan to implement the listed ideas by providing the right incentives (should be age appropriate) to help develop their sense of discipline.

Record the child's responses:

- ....
....

- ....
....

- ....
....

Review: Has it been working? How can you make it better?

- ....
  ....

- ....
  ....

- ....
  ....

Resilience/confidence

Another necessary value or quality for children is a mindset which does not recognise such thing as a 'failure', but sees this as a lesson or feedback.

This is an approach that leads to success in life, and children are actually born with this built into them. I was always amazed at how our three children learned to walk. They tried, they stumbled, they tried again, they fell down, and tried again. They did not give up. They kept on trying until they successfully walked. Isn't this what we call determination, perseverance and/or resilience?

Children should be helped to realise that in life we all stumble sometimes, just like a baby learning to walk. It is not a matter of *if* but *when*. When these difficult moments arrive, it will be their ability to bounce back and try again, and again, and again, until they succeed, that will be the key to their breakthrough in life.

How many times will the baby try to walk before they finally give up trying at all? The answer is: there is no limit. They have to try until they walk. So it is in life – we only truly fail when we stop trying again and give up instead.

One of the best things parents can encourage in their children is this sense of resilience, the elasticity to bounce back quickly from difficult moments and carry on with perseverance and tenacity in the face of adversity.

A good start may be to urge your children to try out this sense of resilience when it comes to maths. They don't have to be told they are clever – your emphasis should be on their resilience, the determination to keep on trying until they get it right.

Closely related to resilience, tenacity, determination, and perseverance is confidence. Confidence is one of the most important ingredients for legendary achievements. The belief and the 'I can do it' mindset is more important than natural abilities or high IQ when it comes to determining achievements.

Confidence generates inner power, the fire within, and stimulates a genuine drive and passion which will make people believe in you.

Confidence, if properly nurtured, will let children see problems as opportunities, setbacks as setups, and failure as a necessary step towards success.

When a child grows up without a sense of resilience/confidence

A child who has not formed this value may lack self-confidence, and have no belief in their ability to bounce back and overcome challenges of life. They are usually afraid of failure, and as a result they often settle for less. They also tend towards self-pity.

How to help your child develop resilience as a value

- Set them a task they may not succeed at on the first attempt. Encourage your child to keep trying until they get it, emphasising that every unsuccessful attempt is not a failure but a useful lesson, or feedback to help you change your approach.

- Encourage autonomy. Let your child dare to fail, and reinforce the idea that when something doesn't work, there is a need to learn from the lesson to try again. We only fail when we stop trying.

- Praise the effort, the demonstration of resilience, and the determination using descriptive praise (refer to **Strategy 6: Using the power of praise** in Chapter 5).

Excellence

Excellence, or the desire to offer the best, highest-quality results, is another indispensable value children should be helped to embrace. The surest route to promotion and success in life is excellence – the mindset to keep improving all the time, to attend to details, and to set high goals.

Wherever there is excellence, it is followed by success. A child with a spirit of excellence will most likely be ahead of another child with talent but without the same spirit.

Within every child is this spirit of excellence. The responsibility of parents is to help the child draw on this latent virtue and make it a habit.

A good start is to pursue excellence in school, by working hard to be 1% better every day than before. This consistent commitment to continuous improvement leads to excellence, which is the hallmark of all great achievements in all spheres of life: education, business, politics, media, sports, government, or science. Children should be taught the importance of continuous, never-ending self-education and self-improvement in their entire being – spirit, soul, and body – so they can equip themselves to excel in life.

Excellence is not synonymous with perfection. Perfection has an element of fear of failure. Excellence, on the other hand, sees failure as a necessary lesson for further improvement.

When a child grows up without a sense of excellence as a value system

Without this as a core value, children do not try hard. They only put in just enough effort so that they will have a certificate, a job, salary, or promotion for themselves. However, those with a strong value system strive to excel so as to serve others. To such value-conscious personalities, nothing justifies mediocrity.

How to help your child develop excellence as a core value

- Set a target to improve on one area of their studies or wider life (for example, maths, or a natural talent such as singing, dancing, playing football, or any other gift to improve a little each time) by working on it daily for a week, a month, or a term.

- Review how they have been doing.

- Move on to another target.

Appreciation

Another must-have value or quality in children is the habit of showing appreciation and gratitude for every little act of kindness and goodwill shown towards them. The habit of saying 'thank you' sincerely from their heart makes both the hearer and the speaker feel better.

Children should be taught that being grateful attracts more of what they are grateful for.

As with all the other values, parents can show the way by modelling it for their children. For example, each family meeting can start with some appreciation.

When a child grows up without a sense of appreciation

Children without a sense of appreciation find it hard to show gratitude to others. 'Thank you' does not appear to be part of their vocabulary, and they are preoccupied primarily with themselves, always pursuing their own self-interest and putting their feelings above everything and everyone else.

How to help your child develop appreciation as a core value

List commendable behaviour or habits your child has been showing:

- ....
....

- ....
....

- ....
....

Offer descriptive praise for each of these (please refer to **Strategy No 6: Using the power of praise**).

Review: Has it been working? How can you make it better?

- ....
....

- ....
....

- ....
....

You can 'nudge' your child to show appreciation. For example, 'Did you notice that ...?'

The child in no time will pick this up and mimic it. When we praise descriptively, children naturally want to do more of whatever has earned them praise.

Attitude

Attitude can be seen as the mindset and feelings a person has about something. This can be positive or negative. Both ways are correct, but each has its path in life. For example, we can see a glass filled to the halfway mark as either half-empty or half-full.

Interestingly, when you calculate the sum of the letters in the word 'attitude', in relation to their position in the 26 letters of the alphabet, it equals *100 [1+20+20+9+20+21+4+5 = 100%]*. This means that the right attitude towards things such as self, other people, private property, money, time, authority, and law and order, is likely to give us 100% in life.

Success and all great achievements start with the right attitude towards yourself. Children should be encouraged to have the right attitude: 'I'm not perfect but I am OK. I'm loved and accepted.' They should aspire to become their best self, improving each day by learning more and more.

The right attitude to money is a must-have. There is nothing inherently bad or evil about money. Money is a tool, which can be used to do good things. But just like any other tool, it can also be used for evil. Teach your children the virtue of saving and investing money, and only spending from the profit from or returns on the money at their disposal (the capital). You may want to use Dr Sunday Adelaja's series on the Laws of Money.[35]

Another important area to look at is the right attitude to time. Time is the resource from which we create everything else in life. Everyone has the same amount: 24 hours in a day. Children should be taught that it's what we do with this treasure called time that determines who we become and what we achieve in

---

[35] See Dr Sunday Adelaja's website, www.sundayadelajablog.com.

this life.

When a child grows up without a sense of good attitude as a value system

Again, without values, children fall back on the default attitude of losers. Instead of living by principles or truths, they become trapped in their own feelings. Feelings exist for a good reason, but living by feelings alone is dangerous. This is because feelings change and are not reliable, while principles are permanent and work for everyone at all times.

The Essential Values for Children in a nutshell

- From a parenting standpoint, core values can be defined as the important guiding principles in life. These are good and desirable principles which form our beliefs, reflect our attitudes, and dictate behaviour.

- Some of the 'must have' values in children are: love, purpose, responsibility, critical thinking, integrity, discipline, excellence, attitude, appreciation, and resilience.

- Values for a child are like the spine for a body. They hold a person together and keep them upright.

- The strength of a child is determined by the strength of their values or value system.

- A child without a value system is just flesh, and they are likely to be driven by emotions, feelings, instincts, and impulses alone, living only the lowest and most animalistic life, and never discovering their true higher self.

- A child with a core value system and who lives by these principles is likely to live a more purposeful and fulfilled life, with external benefits for their family, community, city, country and the world at large.

- Values are to be intentionally taught in an organised fashion, so that children can absorb and pattern their lives after their parents' example.

Notes

Chapter 7: Parenting Tips

In this chapter, you will be introduced to:

- Age-specific parenting tips

  - o The formative years: 0-2 years old

  - o The exploratory years: 2-4 years old

  - o The competence years: 4-7 years old

  - o The independent years: 7-10 years old

  - o The early pubescent years: 10-13 years old

  - o The rollercoaster years: 13-17 years

  - o The early adult years: 18 and over

- Common parenting challenges and scenarios, and how to respond to them

  - o Scenario 1: If your 9-10 year old child physically hits you, what should you do?

  - o Scenario 2: If your 2-year-old child physically hits you, what should you do?

  - o Scenario 3: If your teenager physically hits you, what should you do?

  - o Scenario 4: If your children says "I hate you"

  - o Scenario 5: When a parent blows up or goes to 'angry land' o What if your child is taking drugs?

.

Age-specific parenting tips

A child is believed to form most of their 'personality' by the age of 5. It is still relatively easy to correct them and train them up to the age of 12, but after this time it can be extremely hard to instil essential values if this has not been intentionally done at an earlier stage.

In fact, parenting can start years before a child is even conceived. Successful parenting requires parenting *ourselves* first, so that we are able to give properly to our children.

The 'one-size-fits-all' approach does not work when it comes to parenting children of different age groups. It is therefore appropriate to draw on the latest knowledge regarding age-groups of children and to highlight their characteristics, their unique needs, and what parents can do to bring out their best at that age. An attempt is made to cover most of the groups below.

The formative years: 0-2 years old
The key peculiarities and needs of children between 0-2 years

- These are often known as the 'toddler' years.

- This is the primary age of development, and the crucial formative years in a child's life.

- These years are the attachment stage – children are still totally dependent on parents for all their needs, including food, clothing, shelter, and love, as they cannot yet talk or walk.

- At this stage, the child is recording what is happening around them in these formative years, and internalising the results within their subconscious.

What to do and how to do it for children between 0-

2 years

- Parents are to provide for the physical needs of the body: food, clothing, shelter, and so forth.

- More importantly, parents are to meet the needs of the 'person' inside the child – the soul and the spirit – by communicating, creating, and maintaining the right ambience or atmosphere around the child. The nature of God or the higher self inside the child will be better nurtured and revealed in an atmosphere of love, peace, joy, and acceptance.

- Speak life, hope, and blessings over the child so that they recognise your voice. This can be done even while the child is in the womb, before they are born.

- Pray and hope for the best for them always.

What to avoid for children between 0-2 years

- These are the years of attachment, so neglect should be avoided, as it causes emotional wounds in the child.

- Avoid anything that disturbs a conducive and peaceful atmosphere, and which might be detrimental to the child's development. This includes:

- violence or fighting around the child,

- shouting,

- excessive noise.

- Again, remember that although the child cannot speak, they are recording everything going on around them into their subconscious.

The exploratory years: 2-4 years old

The key peculiarities and needs of children between 2-4 years

- These are the exploratory years, the age of curiosity. Children begin to ask questions, particularly 'why' questions.

- Children of this age want to explore their identity. They demand recognition and do not want to be seen as a toddler anymore.

- They express difficult emotions in negative ways, for the most part.

- They may come across as rebellious.

- They may shout 'No!' to commands by parents.

- Just like the toddler age, they are recording everything as their senses become more active.

- Children of this age experiment and take risks. This is a crucial time – parents can either facilitate the child's quest to be brave, or shut them down by being overly-protective and feeding fear and timidity. A balance needs to be found between allowing your child to explore and take reasonable risks, versus protecting them against harm.

What to do and how to do it for children between 2-4 years

- Allow them the freedom to be creative, explore and take reasonable risks. Only intervene if there is danger of harm.

- Children learn best when satisfying their curiosity. From the age of 3, expose them to a range of learning activities, such as sports, music, gymnastics, swimming, cartons, or purposeful and creative games, to help release the creativity inside themselves.

- The age of 3 onwards is the best time to start to intentionally teach the essential values covered in Chapter 6.

- Create time to play with the child, listen to them, and answer their questions, as a way of showing your love. Also use this one-to-one time to teach values to your child.

- Pray and hope for the best for them always.

What to avoid for children between 2-4 years

- Avoid dictating to them. Instead, allow them to start to choose for themselves in matters concerning their dress, food, games, and so on. Please refer to **Strategy No 5: Empowering your child by giving the chance to choose.**

- Avoid over-protection. Allow them to fall, and allow reasonable accidents, as an important part of self-discovery and the growing-up process. This helps them to learn to be resilient, and also conditions them not to be timid.

The competence years: 4-7 years old
The key peculiarities and needs of children between 4-7 years

- These are the years of acquiring competence. Children

continue to follow their curiosity by learning more about themselves, their abilities, and gifts, and may naturally gravitate towards their passion and purpose.

- Children of this age need self-expression.

- They look for friends, and want to spend more time with friends (sleepovers, etc.).

- They express feelings, but may not yet fully understand how to best express difficult feelings.

What to do and how to do it for children between 4-7 years

- Allow them the freedom to explore and the freedom to choose. Please refer to **Strategy No 5: Empowering your child by giving the chance to choose** for more.

- Let them play frequently with friends you can trust.

- Continue teaching the essential values covered in Chapter 6.

- Affirm them and their uniqueness using Descriptive Praise (please refer to **Strategy No 6: Use the power of praise**).

- Teach them how to express their difficult and negative feelings, such as fear, frustration, and anger, emphasising the effect this may have on other peoples' feelings.

- Teach them appreciation and to say 'thank you' and 'please'.

- Pray and hope for the best for them always.

What to avoid for children between 4-7 years

- Avoid forcing things on them – instead, give them the freedom to choose.

- Avoid being overly protective.

The independent years: 7-10 years old

The key peculiarities and needs of children between 7-10 years

- Children of this age recognise other authorities in their life: friends, celebrities, teachers, heroes.

- They need more parental love and attention, so that this place is not taken by other less healthy 'authorities'.

- They seek more independence.

- They begin to question their identity, and some may opt for gender/sex change.

What to do and how to do it for children between 7-10 years

- They need more unconditional love, acceptance, and other related gifts.

- Allow them the freedom to try things, while coaching them as they go. Try to strike the right balance between freedom and being 'controlling' (refer to **Strategy No 5: Empowering your child by giving the chance to choose**).

- Get them busy in productive extra-curricular activities, such as sports, music, drama, and so on.

- Continue teaching them the values covered in Chapter 6.

- Pray and hope for the best for them always.

What to avoid for children between 7-10 years

- Avoid neglecting them. Some of them may, as a result of a lack of love and acceptance from parents and guardians, begin to question themselves and in their vulnerability seek answers from the wrong places and people.

- This is usually the period when children begin to question their gender identity.

- Avoid being controlling and coercive.

The early pubescent years: 10-13 years old
The key peculiarities and needs of children between 10-13 years

- This is the critical final window when it is relatively easy to instil values and influence children positively. After 13, this becomes more difficult.

- These are years characterised by concerns about themselves, about others, and about issues in general. They begin to doubt if they are good enough, beautiful enough, and so on.

- They now approach puberty and adolescence, when they will notice changes in their physical bodies. They become more conscious about their self-image.

- Boys may begin to show more signs of rebellion, and the girls may show mood swings.

- They seek relationships, and become more aware of their sexuality.

What to do and how to do it for children between 10-13 years

- Be their friend. Confide in them so they can also confide in you, having felt your authenticity.

- Let them know that their identity is not in their body.

- Continue teaching the core values covered in Chapter 6.

- Pray and hope for the best for them always.

What to avoid for children between 10-13 years

- Avoid being a commander who is always ordering them about.

- Avoid blaming them, instead of addressing the issues at hand.

The rollercoaster years: 13-17 years old
The key peculiarities and needs of children between 13-17 years

- These are the years when children are at the height of puberty/adolescence, and they develop more intimacy with parents or other people.

- They are on a teenage emotional rollercoaster at this time. They experience hormonal changes as an interplay of the brain, emotions, and biochemistry, which together create the chemicals responsible for their behaviour.

- They express their sexuality. Some have their 'first love' or 'first crush'.

- They need more unconditional love, so parents should be their best friend, taking care to treat them as equals.

- They may withdraw into themselves when they are at home.

- They are at the height of either building more confidence or doubt in themselves, constantly wondering if they are 'adequate'.

- They may show signs of stubbornness.

- The influence of the internet and social media may add to the pressure and their feeling of inadequacy.

- They worry about their image and appearance, and if they fit in socially.

- Pray and hope for the best for them always.

What to do and how to do it for children between 13-17 years

- Become their friend, or else they may want to hang out with other less positive friends.

- Be a role model. Model the essential values covered in Chapter 6. They may want to see these values *shown* to them rather than *said* to them.

- Help them to root their identity in the 'invisible', knowing that they are the image of God and that there is no need for them to seek their identity from someone else, whether it be the media, celebrities, or friends.

- Allow them to find out things for themselves. Get them busy doing things aligned with their gifts, passion and purpose.

- Allow them to ask questions.

- Allow them to make mistakes and learn from their mistakes, except where they are at risk of doing significant harm to themselves and/or others. This allows them to learn resilience, problem-solving skills, and confidence. Encourage them to see mistakes as essential opportunity for growth.

- Parents should make their teenagers aware that the hormonal changes they are experiencing are not because they are bad people, but a natural phenomenon that will pass and will not last forever.

- Educate teenagers about the benefits and dangers of social media, the internet, and online friendships. Also highlight the dangers of drug and alcohol abuse, pornography, gambling, bad company, and so on.

- Involve them in decisions that affect them (refer to **Strategy No 7: Problem-solving skills**).

- Pray and hope for the best for them always.

What to avoid for children between 13-17 years

- Avoid giving commands and demanding obedience.

- Avoid doing things for them. Let them try – if they fail, help them learn from the experience, and try again until they can succeed at anything they do.

- Avoid lashing out at them with angry words and

accusations, such as 'you are rude'. Please refer here to **Strategy No 1: Separate the 'Who' from the 'Do'.**

- Don't compare them with anyone; instead, celebrate their uniqueness.

- Don't push them.

The early adult years: 18 and over
The key peculiarities and needs of children over 18

- They are now adults and will demand to be treated that way.

- They are about to leave home for college, a career, or a partner, or to join the 'rat race' if they have not discovered their purpose and something greater than themselves to live for.

- The key is to have instilled the essential values in them by now, so that you can let them go in full confidence and assurance.

- They want their feelings to be acknowledged, and their views to be respected.

- They want honesty and authenticity from guardians.

What to do and how to do it for children over 18

- Treat them as equals.

- Take them more seriously.

- Be willing to let them go and accept that they are no longer obliged to take your advice.

- You may only offer suggestions.

- You may influence them through mentorship, as a friend.

- Pray and hope for the best for them always.

What to avoid for children over 18

- Avoid any attempt to treat them like a child, although s/he will always be your child.

- Never lash out at them.

Common parenting challenges and scenarios, and how to respond to them

Scenario 1: If your 9-year-old child physically hits you, what should you do?

This shows that something is fundamentally wrong, and the root cause of this behaviour must be identified and addressed. How, where and why did the child become like that?

This can be approached in many ways. Here are three options:

a) The easiest approach, and the one most parents take, is to see the child as an enemy, becoming cross and reacting emotionally to the trigger. This results in lashing out at the child in return.

b) An alternative reaction could be, 'You hit me? That's bad and you will face the consequences.' Then you punish the child in some way.

c) A final approach is to acknowledge the child's feelings, describing the action without accusing or blaming them, and then (when calm) state your expectations:

- 'I was hit. It appears you were unhappy about something, you were angry.'

- 'I expect you to express that anger in another way: you can hit the floor, the wall, something, but not me. Human beings are not for hitting.'

Options 'a' and 'b' fail to address the problem. They merely react to it. Option 'a' will actually make the problem worse, whereas 'b' is relatively better, but children may react negatively to any form of punishment and may not learn from it.

Option 'c' is the best course of action and the one most likely to be effective. It teaches the child by modelling how to control their emotions. Option 'a' in particular only makes the parents become just as bad as the child, in an attempt to correct a child's inability to properly express their emotions.

Scenario 2: If your 2-year-old child physically hits you, what should you do?

Like Scenario 1, the best approach here is to validate, accept, and acknowledge the feelings, but not the action. You should also actually model to the child what is expected from them next time.

- First, you need to protect yourself from getting hurt, and wait until the trigger has subsided. It helps if you take deep breaths.

- Show empathy to the child by hugging or touching them, and say 'I can see how frustrated you are.'

- Explain to them, 'It's fine to be upset but it's not okay to express it by hitting me. Human beings are not for hitting.'

- Warn them, 'Next time, it's okay to express your feelings by crying, stamping, or jumping, but not hitting another person, as this hurts them.'

- You may even brainstorm with the child some options for harmlessly expressing the feelings next time, by asking: 'What are some of the other ways you can express your anger without hitting someone: any ideas?' When they have given you some, you can also add other options:

'What about kicking your football?' Then ask, 'Which one of these will work better for you?'

Scenario 3: If your teenager physically hits you, what should you do?

First, you need to protect yourself from getting hurt, and wait until your child has calmed down. A teenager can do real harm to a parent, even unintentionally.

Then, in addition to the best responses from Scenarios 1 and 2, you may want to reflect if you yourself played any part in making your teenager upset. If this is the case, then a good starting point when there is calm is to take full responsibility and apologise. For example:

- 'I am sorry I did… or said… , and that made you angry.'

- 'However, next time I would appreciate if you could find another way to express your anger, rather than hit me.'

- 'That really hurts, and it's unacceptable.'

Scenario 4: If your child says 'I hate you'

'I hate you' is a sentence no parent wants to hear. It can have a devastating effect on us all. A survey of teenagers reveals that in one year, a typical teenager says 'I hate you' 27 times to their parents, and shouts at them 59 times.[36]

---

[36] From the Daily Mail, 'Teens shout at parents 59 times a year…' http://www.dailymail.co.uk/femail/article-2585465/Parents-teens-shouted-59-TIMES-year-worries-no-one-fancies-just-wanting-normal.html.

Why do children say such a potentially destructive thing to the people they are supposed to love most?

Teenagers may be driven by hormonal changes, among other things. Younger children may not have developed the ability and the vocabulary to positively articulate their strong feelings, for example when parents say 'No' or prevent them from having or doing their favourite things, such as toys and games.

So a good response from an emotionally-intelligent parent is not to take it as a personal attack. Instead, follow an intentional process of acknowledging the child's feelings, and show them how to express such difficult feelings, like this:

- 'You must be very angry.' (This must be said showing empathy)

- 'When I hear such statements, they make me feel really bad and hurt.'

- 'I would be glad if you could find a more calm and acceptable way to express your feelings.'

- 'What do you think?'

Here, you may invite the child to suggest ideas and then choose the best and most practical one. This may not work in the heat of the moment, in which case parents are advised to first regulate their own emotions, and wait until the right time, when everyone is calm, before trying to address the issue.

Scenario 5: When a parent blows up or goes to 'angry land'

Parents also lose their temper sometimes. This is perfectly normal. When parents are angry, the logical side of the brain shuts down, and the 'child' inside takes over. Accusatory and blame-filled statements like these can be heard: 'You did it again? How many times do I have to tell you? Are you really so dumb?'

The beauty of parenting is that parents always get a second chance. So pause, take a deep breath, and withdraw, saying 'I cannot talk more right now...'

When you are calm, having processed and reflected on what happened, go back to your child and say, 'I have thought about what I said the other day. I really didn't mean to ...... This is what I wanted to say ....' And concentrate on saying what you mean in the best way.

What if your child is taking drugs?

- This is beyond the scope this book. Parents may consider seeking professional advice in these cases.

- Professional advice is also recommended for children with special needs, such as:

    o Dyslexia

    o Attention Deficit Hyperactivity Disorder (ADHD)

    o Down's syndrome

    o Multiple sclerosis

For more scenarios and suggestions

Please visit my website, where you will find updates, tips and links: www.livingyourbest.co.uk.

Notes

Closing Thoughts

Parenting is one of the toughest jobs in the world. In spite of the difficulty involved, many parents start out on this journey without any preparation.

My own story clearly shows how ill-equipped I was in the early stages of parenting. If I can learn about and attain a certain degree of mastery at this vocation, I am of the firm view that any parent can also do it, if you only make a sincere attempt.

The two main ideas I would like you to take away from this book are:

- You need the desire to learn while on this job.

- You need the commitment to pay the price for putting new knowledge into practice, as these ideas only work when we become good at using them.

My main objective is to equip parents to intentionally train their children to discover themselves and live by a strong set of values. If you do this, your children will not merely react to events in life, but take charge of and full responsibility for their lives.

There are very useful ideas included here, from Chapter 1 right through to the end, that parents can pick up and implement straight away. I would particularly like you to return to the **7 strategies**:

1. Separate the 'Who' from the 'Do'

2. Look after yourself first

3. Lead by example

4. Let your child feel heard and listened to

5. Empower your child by giving them the chance to choose

6. Use the power of praise

7. Teach problem-solving skills

This is a non-exhaustive list, but it represents some of the most practical and useful tips parents can have to hand, and they can all be put into action straight away.

This book combines ideas from the field of psychology, at the heart of which is using emotional intelligence as the key to ensuring cooperation from your children, and instilling values to help your children discover their true self. In this way, they will live for a cause greater than themselves, to the lasting benefit of humanity as a whole.

Finally, I can assure you that the principles in this book work. They have been working for the parents who have tried them. The practical stories I have included here are a demonstration of how effective these ideas and techniques are in action.

It has been my hope and pleasure to inspire others through my writing. I was thrilled when I received the following feedback from parents who had read the very first draft of Chapter 1 of this book:

> 'Hi John
>
> I thought the introduction was really interesting and I would buy your book to read the rest of it. Your story made me cry and I was a sobbing mess when I got off the train. I didn't know you went through such a terrible ordeal a few years ago and I'm glad things were resolved in the end.
>
> I think you are right in pointing out that because of the Act, parenting is different for the current generation of

parents. We are the generation caught in between as we were brought up being caned, but now we have to bring up our children without the cane.

Chapter 1 was thought provoking and has made me reflect more on what parenting means.

I wish you all the best with the book. And you have to let me know when it is out!'

'Hello John

This book needs to be every parent and career's holy book. Thank you for being selfless and empowering us with your personal experience and this Fantastic book, I could feel the lovely pure heart from which the book was written. I am sure this book will inspire many parents, like it inspired Yaw and I. I believe many children will have better childhood experience from their parents and careers because of your selflessness. I believe this world will have a much better future generation because of this book. I can't wait to have my own copy to add to my library collection and share with loved ones!'

The third comment I received simply read:

'Every parent needs to read this. It is already changing me. The shouting has stopped.'

I have never had a more powerful affirmation of the importance of what I am doing.

I must congratulate you, again, for taking the effort to read this book. It makes all the labour worthwhile when we can look to the future with confidence, and expect good outcomes for our children. All you need to do is implement the lessons and the skills in this book, and don't give up!

It is my utmost hope that you live long enough to see the reward of your efforts and hard work, and that your children will one day notice the effort you have put into raising them. I am sure that when they do, they will thank you for having, at the very least, tried your best.

Good luck!

Goal-setting Template

What do I want? (State the goal clearly, making it specific)	Why do I want this?	What can I do every day to move a step towards achieving the goal?	How and by when do I want to achieve this goal?

Acknowledgements

Dr Sunday Adelaja (DSA): Thank you for being a mentor to me. You taught me the fundamental concept of conversion, that our spiritual experiences are meaningless unless they are converted into tangible forms to benefit other people. This book is evidence of that concept.

Rev Edwin Donkor (ICGC Regional overseer, Europe and America)**:** You have been like a father to me. I have yet to see anyone of your stature who has a similar extraordinary sense of wisdom and humility.

Louis Kwabena Anane: You have been inspiring me since 1994. You are a true friend. Thank you for your review of this manuscript, with comments that gave me much healthy food for thought.

Peter Frimpong Manso: Thank you for your review and your scholarly suggestions, which made me think and approach things differently.

Poh Leng: Thank you for your insightful and encouraging feedback from a parent's perspective.

Maria Paler: You are a star. I appreciate your useful comments on the story.

Nkiru Ojimadu: Thank you for getting me started and inspiring me with your Bestseller achievement.

Everyone: I want to say thank you to anyone who has supported me and contributed to this project in any way, shape or form – whether you bought this book or a product, visited my website, or subscribed to my updates. Without you, my readers and supporters, I would not be here. You are the reason that I can continue this worthwhile project.

About the Author

John has been an educator in higher education in the United Kingdom for more than 7 years. He currently teaches Economics on pathway programmes at Newcastle University London. His teaching excellence recently earned him the title of pathway teacher of the year 2018.

In addition to his professional ACCA qualification, he holds a Master's Degree in Economics of Globalisation and European Integration, awarded by a consortium of nine global universities.

He has discovered his purpose in life, and has a genuine passion to share this with the world, to make life a little better for everyone.

As parents, John and Linda have raised three thriving children. They are still constantly learning and turning their knowledge and experience into strategies and tools to help parents on their own journey, and to be advocates for both children and their guardians. He has actually been sharing the success principles he has discovered with people in his book(s), workshops, and seminars.

For speaking engagements, please do contact him at John.Adjei@livingyourbest.co.uk or learn more about him at www.livingyourbest.co.uk

Lastly, if you found this book useful, I would really appreciate if you could post a short review on Amazon using the link below. Your support makes enormous difference, and this incredibly helps other parents and guardians out there. I personally read all your reviews so I can get your feedback to make this book even better.

Please click or type " **geBook.at/AmazonJA** "   to your browser and scroll down to Customer reviews.

Thanks   again   for   your   support.

Index

43356209R00121

Printed in Poland
by Amazon Fulfillment
Poland Sp. z o.o., Wrocław